# Virginia Woolf

## Mary Ann Caws

THE OVERLOOK PRESS
WOODSTOCK & NEW YORK

First published in paperback in the United States in 2004 by
The Overlook Press, Peter Mayer Publishers, Inc.
Woodstock & New York

WOODSTOCK:
One Overlook Drive
Woodstock, NY 12498
www.overlookpress.com
[For individual orders, bulk and special sales, contact our Woodstock office]

NEW YORK:
141 Wooster Street
New York, NY 10012

Copyright © 2001 Mary Ann Caws

All Rights Reserved. No part of this publication may be reproduced or
transmitted in any form or by any means, electronic or mechanical, including
photocopy, recording, or any information storage and retrieval system now
known or to be invented without permission in writing from the publisher,
except by a reviewer who wishes to quote brief passages in connection with
a review written for inclusion in a magazine, newspaper, or broadcast.

Published by arrangement with Penguin Books Ltd.

Library of Congress Cataloging-in-Publication Data

Caws, Mary Ann.
Virginia Woolf / Mary Ann Caws.
p. cm.
Includes bibliographical references.
1. Woolf, Virginia, 1882-1941. 2. Novelists, English—20th century—Biography.
3. Women and literature—England—History—20th century. I. Title.
PR6045.O72 Z568 2002    823'.912—b21    2002523056

Printed in Singapore
9 8 7 6 5 4 3 2 1
ISBN 1-58567-520-2

# Contents

*Acknowledgements*   vii

VIRGINIA WOOLF

Making Scenes   1

Early Times: Hyde Park Gate and St Ives   3

Bloomsbury's London   13

Monk's House, Hogarth House and Charleston   27

Auppegard, Roquebrune and Cassis   41

Virginia and Vita   62

Travelling with Leonard and also with Roger   71

Virginia Woolf and Her Mind   79

Virginia Woolf: Reader and Writer   91

Virginia and Bloomsbury   97

Closer: Virginia's Expressing Herself   112

Leaving: the Ouse   120

*Chronology*   127
*Bibliography*   130
*List of Illustrations*   132

# Acknowledgements

First of all, my 'from always' friend Sarah Bird Wright invited me to share in her experience of Monk's House when she was renting it. I was given Virginia Woolf's bedroom, and my children, Leonard's study. Bathing in the tub provided by the proceeds from *Mrs Dalloway*, dining at the table where so much conversation had transpired, walking in the garden and playing bowls there, as the visitors to Monk's House are seen doing in this book: it was all pre-inspiration for my *Women of Bloomsbury: Virginia, Vanessa, and Carrington*, published by Routledge in 1989, for which the great Frances Partridge was an unending resource and vital help.

When Sarah Bird Wright and I wrote our *Bloomsbury and France: Art and Friends* of 1997 (published by Oxford University Press in the USA and the UK and dedicated to Frances Partridge), we had the inestimable help of Quentin Bell, Angelica Garnett, Henrietta Garnett, Carolyn Heilbrun, Alice Mauron and Nigel Nicolson, as well as my cousin Deborah Gage. Each of those friends is to be thanked also, directly and indirectly, for the present volume, which continues from there.

The observations and patience of my various editors and picture researchers, in particular those of Caroline Pretty – who initiated this series – were invaluable. My thanks to Anna South for her original interest. Annette Fern of the Houghton Library at Harvard and her associates were helpful and long-suffering. My thanks to everyone, named and not, who has aided in the production of this volume.

Mary Ann Caws
*New York and Provence,*
*October 2000 and August 2001*

'It goes too quick – too quick. If only one could sip slowly
& relish every grain of every hour!' (Diary 2, p. 128)

'I don't believe in aging. I believe in forever altering one's
aspect to the sun. Hence my optimism' (Diary 4, p. 125)

# VIRGINIA WOOLF

## *Making Scenes*

Virginia Woolf found her visual memory to be her own natural way of representing the past. The creation or recreation of a scene seemed to her what would best endure in her writing (*Moments of Being*, p. 122). Following her lead, this brief illustrated life of Virginia Woolf is itself based on visual scenes: the representations of her friends, her surroundings, and herself that best depict her way of being, the places and the people that mattered to her. These images are far more than decorative props: they are where this project started, for I have tried to visualize her life before writing it.

> But for a moment I had sat on the turf somewhere high above the flow of the sea and the sounds of the woods, and had seen the house, the garden, and the waves breaking. The old nurse who turns the pages of the picture-book had stopped and had said, 'Look. This is the truth' (The Waves, p. 287).

What appears true to sight may be no less true to insight; that is my hope for these pages.

*A formal family gathering. Back row: Gerald Duckworth, Virginia, Thoby and Vanessa Stephen, Geor[ge] Duckworth; front row: Adrian, Juli[a] and Leslie Stephen.*

# Early Times: Hyde Park Gate and St Ives

Virginia Woolf was born in 1882, to Julia Duckworth Stephen and her enormously learned husband, Leslie Stephen, when her parents were thirty-six and fifty respectively; her elder sister Vanessa had been born in 1879. The London family home at 22 Hyde Park Gate was rather a dark place, tall, narrow, six floors high, with a gloomy interior. The air was, and the house also, thick with things, objects of all sorts, as was any Victorian parlour. Living in this atmosphere was a large number of people, cared for by seven servants. Besides their parents, there were Virginia and Vanessa's brothers Adrian (whom Julia called 'My Joy') and Thoby, whom Virginia greatly admired and loved, and Laura, Leslie Stephen's slightly retarded daughter, from his former marriage to Minny Thackeray, whose repeated breakdowns, and eventual institutionalization seemed to preface Virginia Woolf's own breakdowns and severe depressions, which occurred in cycles throughout her life. There were also Julia's three children from her first marriage to Herbert Duckworth: George, Stella (who was to marry Jack Hills) and Gerald. George and Gerald, respectively fourteen and twelve years older than Virginia, were handsome, easy-going, and prompt to take liberties, psychological and physical, with both girls. George was tall and, as Virginia told it, abnormally stupid.

In her 'Sketch of the Past', she describes Gerald exploring her private parts, in front of the looking-glass outside the dining room, when she was quite small. The memory was very strong, unforgettable. He had perched her on a ledge: 'I remember resenting, disliking it', and she adds a dream in which 'a horrible face – the face of an animal – suddenly showed over my shoulder' (*Moments*, p. 69). George was prone to fondling her as she bent over her Greek lessons, she writes to Vanessa, and to invade her bedroom, telling her

**Left**  Virginia at twenty, 1902.
The most frequently reproduced of all her portraits, even
making a wall appearance in
the sitcom Murphy Brown.

**Right**  Vanessa Bell's portrait
of Virginia Woolf, 1912. The
portrait captures just the tilt of
Virginia's head and the posture
that makes the face not essential: no painting of Virginia
Woolf has ever rendered her
more profoundly. 'You do know
really how much you help me
… I couldn't get on at all if it
weren't for you' (Letters, 6,
p. 211).

to fear nothing (*Letters* 1, p. 472). Scarcely the way to drive out fear.
It is symptomatic of his behaviour that once, when she had made
a green dress, he commanded her to 'go and tear it up'. All of this
was often thought to have been one of the causes of Virginia's frequent mental disturbances that were to plague her all her life, and,
less crucially, of some of her misgivings about her appearance. In
1926, she proclaimed that she was 'giving up the hope of being well
dressed'. Her sense of her awkwardness contrasted with her sense
of her mother's great beauty. The concrete image of this was the
looking-glass, in which she caught her image, and, like the wearer
of 'The New Dress', would frequently be ashamed of the sight. If
she so hated shopping for new clothes, even for underwear, it was

part of this discomfort with her own image. Many of the portraits and photographs we have of her depict this same feeling: it is perhaps her sister Vanessa's faceless portrait of Virginia that best captures her.

With all these men around, she and her sister became very close conspirators: 'Coming and going, we formed our private nucleus.

There we were, alone, with Father all day. In the evening Adrian would come back from Westminster; then Jack from Lincoln's Inn; then Gerald from Dent's or Henrietta Street; then George from the Post Office or the Treasury; and Thoby would be at Clifton or at Cambridge. The staple day would be a day spent together. And therefore we made together a small world inside the big world.' And from the same vantage point. In this richly atmospheric world of Hyde Park Gate, the sisters printed their own newspaper about family goings-on, real and

*The Stephens and their younger daughter Virginia at Talland Hous[e] the St Ives house so beloved of them all. 'Life so new. People so enchanting. The sound of the sea at night' (Diary 2, p. 103).*

imagined. They were close in this, as in all things. Again and again, in Virginia's crises of illness and madness – often the same thing for her – it was Vanessa who was her closest comfort until Leonard took over that responsibility. There is throughout Virginia's entire life a feeling of desirousness, of real neediness, in all her communications with Vanessa. With others also, but especially with Vanessa, whose reassurance was constantly needed, even as her steadiness and parenting were the no-less-frequent cause of envy and of interior grief, over what she once was to call 'Nessa's overwhelming supremacy' (*Diary* 3, p. 323). Angelica Garnett, Vanessa's daughter, was to speak of Vanessa's 'emotional presence equalled by no one else' (Garnett, *The Eternal Moment*, p.10).

So used was Virginia to sharing her moods with her sister that each high point of ecstasy called for sisterly communion (*Letters* 6, p. 158): 'And as usual I thought of you. Do you think we have the same pair of eyes, only different spectacles? I rather think I'm more nearly attached to you than sisters should be. Why is it I never stop thinking of you?' Vanessa would always understand her moods and inclinations: 'A bubbly rapture in Fitzroy Street. I must ask Nessa why we are so happy' (*Diary* 4, p. 30). These surges of joy were part of Virginia's definition of herself always, whether in their establishment at Fitzroy Street, or later at Brunswick Square or Mecklenburgh Square.

Against the winter gloom and the complicated dark interior of Hyde Park Gate, there were the summers in the Cornish seaside village of St Ives full of a simple light. Leslie Stephen had found Talland House, the family home in St Ives, in 1881, and lived with his family there in the summer. It was (and is) a steep-hilled noisy town, with its bustling fish market, and its high-windowed houses.

It was at St Ives that Virginia had her first recollection of her mother's dress. The sight of red and purple flowers there on a black background filled her vision as the foundation of her past and of her ongoing life. Lying in her bed in the St Ives nursery, as she recounts it in the celebrated slim volume, *Moments of Being*, she had an equally strong aural memory:

*It is of hearing the waves breaking, one, two, one, two, and*
*seeing a splash of water over the beach, and then breaking,*
*one, two, one, two, behind a yellow blind. It is of hearing*
*the blind draw its little cord across the floor as the wind blew*
*the blind out. It is of lying and hearing this splash and seeing*
*this light, and feeling, it is almost impossible that I should be*
*here; of feeling the purest ecstasy I can conceive* (Moments,
p. 64).

But even before Julia died in 1895, they had decided not to return
to Talland House, because the view towards the bay was cut off by
the building of the Porthminster Hotel. So the summer idyll ended.
That loss, irretrievable except in memory and the writing it nourished, led to one of the simplest and most grief-laden phrases in
Woolf's writings: 'And St Ives vanished for ever' (*Moments*, p.117).
When, in a sketch preparatory for *The Waves*, Woolf draws on a
similar echo of seaside light, we are reminded of what St Ives
stood for in her mind: a sea, a garden, and dawn breaking: 'The
light quickens. The garden. The garden' (Lee, *Virginia Woolf*, p. 24).

Of course, the Godrevy Lighthouse at St Ives shines its own
beam in *To the Lighthouse*, but the image in the mind gives a still
more powerful light: 'To have our own house; our own garden,
to have the Bay; the sea; the moors … to hear the
waves breaking that first night behind the yellow
blind; to dig in the sand; to go sailing in a fishing
boat; to scrabble over the rocks …' (*Moments*,
p. 30). The children spent their time gloriously,
moth hunting, and hunting up all the names in
books on butterflies and moths. In her diary, Woolf retells again the
Cornwall experience, when life seemed so fresh, everything seemed
so new, and she could hear the sea at night (*Diary* 2, p. 103).

*Virginia and Vanessa Stephen at*
*St Ives. Virginia always delighted*
*her sister's company: 'I instinctive*
*want someone to catch my overfl*
*of pleasure' (Diary 2, p. 129).*

All her life, Woolf was to value what she referred to as Thomas
Hardy's 'moments of vision', that kind of romanticized intensity
that makes the instant blaze. The condensed two and a half
months in Talland House were so pungent in her memory that
later, after finding a sufficiently romantic house near Lewes, she

called it Little Talland House. Her description of Talland House obviously draws on an echo of Proust's memorable garden gate, with its 'timid, oval, golden' bell that Swann would ring on those Sundays rich with a basket of raspberries under the large-branched chestnut tree (Proust, *In Search of Lost Time* 1, p. 14). At St Ives, she remembered a hot summer day, when the lawn was scattered with tea tables laden with 'great bowls of strawberries and cream' (*Moments*, p. 86). The correspondence implicitly called on creates, for the readers of both authors, a shared memory, prolonging the sound and making the imagined sight more intimate: 'You entered Talland house by a large wooden gate, the sound of whose latch clicking comes back; you went up the carriage drive, with its steep wall scattered with mesembryanthemums' (*Moments*, p. 111).

***Right*** *Vanessa Bell's dust jackets of* To the Lighthouse *(1927) – the story of Mrs Ramsay, beautiful an dead so young, and her philosoph husband, modelled on Virginia's parents – and* Mrs Dalloway *(192 – Clarissa Dalloway's London day choosing flowers for her party, wh prolongs her past into her present.*

From this moment, she felt ecstasy in these memories. Later, she felt those same memories gaining in complexity and losing in strength (*Moments*, p. 67). The writer's self-consciousness as viewer repeatedly invaded her mind. The images she uses for her own awkwardness recur in a series of complex intertwinings. What was never complicated was her feeling for her mother and her mother's beauty. Julia Duckworth was, behind her definite profile, silent and sad, yet no less quick and active, and central to the whole atmosphere of the Stephen home, so much so that it was difficult, if not impossible, to grasp her 'as a whole thing. Talland house was full of her; Hyde Park Gate was full of her … She was keeping what I call in my shorthand the panoply of life – that which we all lived in common – in being' (*Moments*, p. 83). Their intimacy was great, and Julia's tenderness manifest. Her last words to Virginia were: 'Hold yourself straight, my little goat' (*Moments*, p. 84). So she was always called 'the Goat'. Yet when Julia died in May 1895, little remained, apparently at least, of the atmosphere she had created. The thirteen-year-old Virginia remembered leaning from the window of her nursery, seeing Dr Seton walk away, his hands clasped behind him, and a flock of pigeons swooping about

and settling in the blue morning. It was springtime then, and that feeling of everything ending stayed with the child Virginia was.

The girls were left to care for the irascible and exigent father, whose affection was great, but whose demands were no less so, particularly in regard to family finances. He would groan loudly at the idea of spending a penny more than he considered enough. Julia's early death was to haunt Virginia until she was forty-four. Walking around Tavistock Square one day, she said, 'I made up, as I sometimes make up my books, *To the Lighthouse*, in a great, apparently involuntary rush. One thing burst into another' (*Moments*, p. 81). With the writing of that elegy to her parents, she had exorcized the most painful part of the memory. When Mrs Ramsay dies, in the central portion of that book, it is between square brackets, as if that death might be somehow elided.

# Bloomsbury's London

After the death of Leslie Stephen, in 1904, of bowel cancer, the sisters and Adrian shared a house, as far removed from the former one as possible, at 46 Gordon Square in London. Virginia began to develop a sense of herself as a writer, claiming, in one of her early notebooks, that such shocks, the way of receiving them, explaining them, and resisting them, was what made one a writer: they were then to be conceived of as valuable. In the new home, the mood was entirely different from that of the previous Victorian dwelling: there was nothing to prevent doing, saying, being whatever one wanted. One could experiment with anything. 'Everything was going to be new; everything was going to be different. Everything was on trial' (*Moments*, p. 201). And together, the sisters rented a lovely house at Asheham, which they occupied until, in 1919, its owner needed it back.

The sisters remained as close as sisters can be. They always shared almost everything: gossip, feelings, friends. Yet the drama of losses continued for Virginia. Two days after their beloved brother Thoby died at twenty-six of typhoid fever, on 20 November 1906, Vanessa accepted Clive Bell's offer of marriage. Missing Thoby, dead so young and so unjustly, Virginia walked around London alone, and 'engaged with' her anguish, fighting it, and her 'dumb rage' over his loss. She had not only lost the brother she most admired – paradoxically for his reserve, almost to the point of aloofness, already a variety of the absent Perceval in *The Waves* – she had also lost Vanessa, her closest friend. She and Adrian had to leave 46 Gordon Square, where the Bells were to live, and moved to 29 Fitzroy Square, close by, before moving to a larger house in Brunswick Square. It was in this

*...inting of 46 Gordon Square, ...09, by Vanessa Bell. The house ...here the Stephen children moved ...on the death of Sir Leslie ...ephen: an experiment in free ...ing, as they saw it. 'So now there ...s nothing that one could not say, ...at one could not do, at 46 Gordon ...uare' (Moments, p. 274).*

Bloomsbury district that most of their friends lived, thus the name of the group.

The gregarious Clive Bell had become connected with Thoby at Trinity College, Cambridge: although he was never a member of the Apostles, that celebrated secret conversation society, he belonged to the Midnight Society instead, for play reading, and was to devote his life to French art and literature; he was also valued as a close friend by many painters, including Picasso. It was often said of him that he could enliven any dinner party and make everyone at it feel intelligent. He had met the sisters with Thoby on their European tour after their father's death, and taken them around Paris. When they married, in 1907, Vanessa was twenty-eight. With Clive, Virginia carried on a jealous flirtation, in great part because of her hurt over the loss of Vanessa.

Vanessa and Clive were to have, in the long run, what we think of as an open marriage. He had had other close relationships, and was to have still closer ones: of Vanessa's relation to the painter Roger Fry, and then to Duncan Grant, he seems not to have been particularly jealous. In 1910, Roger Fry had met Clive and Vanessa on a train between Cambridge and London, and they became immediate friends. Vanessa and Roger had gone with Clive and Harry Norton, a Cambridge mathematician, to Turkey in the spring of 1911; Vanessa had had a miscarriage and breakdown, was nursed back to health by Roger, and the two fell in love. The affair lasted until 1913; thereafter, Vanessa's affections shifted towards the personable, handsome and homosexual Duncan Grant, whose talent at painting she admired far above Roger's — a not inconsiderable factor in the situation, given Vanessa's passion for art. She and Duncan would live and work together the rest of their lives, despite Vanessa's distress over Duncan's lovers, in particular David [Bunny] Garnett.

After Roger was no longer so involved with her sister, Virginia found her own relationship with him to be closer. They would, forever, argue over art and literature, structure and texture, over

*Left: Early photograph of Virginia Stephen in Cornwall, 1916 (capturing her sideways glance, at once shy and seductive).*

*Overleaf Leonard Woolf, Roger Fry and Virginia Woolf, 1912. Virginia with the two most important men in her life after her father's death.*

Shakespeare and the poets they both loved. Virginia was always to admire Roger greatly, and in particular his enthusiasm for all sorts of things, his ebullient being. He was exuberance itself, and her writer's mind, as well as her insatiable curiosity, had delighted in everything about him, from the moment they met, in 1910. 'So Roger appeared. He appeared, I seem to think, in a large ulster coat, every pocket of which was stuffed with a book, a paint box or something intriguing: special tips which he had bought from a little man in the back street; he had canvases under his arms; his hair flew; his eyes glowed' (Caws and Wright, *Bloomsbury and France*, p. 303).

After Vanessa's marriage to Clive, Virginia was less reluctant to marry Leonard Woolf, who had proposed previously. He had been stationed in Ceylon; his hands trembled ceaselessly – because of signing death warrants, it is said – and Virginia called him 'a penniless Jew' (*Letters* 1, p. 500). The ironic accent falls on 'penniless' because of the contemporary myth of the richness of the Hebrew establishment, according to Carolyn Heilbrun [in conversation with the author], so that Virginia was claiming for him, as she always would for herself, an outsider's status. As Virginia wrote to Leonard: 'Your being a Jew ... you seem so foreign' (*Letters* 1, p. 496).

Leonard was everything to Virginia. He was thirty-three, and Virginia thirty, when they married in St Pancras Town Hall, at 12.15 p.m. on Saturday, 10 August 1912. Clive, with whom Virginia had flirted after Vanessa's marriage, wrote her a note: 'I love you very much and I love your lover too' (Lee, *Virginia Woolf*, p. 322). And lovers they were, more in the spiritual sense of the word than the physical; but it was no less deep. Leonard had a dry precision which could verge on the austere. For Virginia's niece, Angelica Garnett, Leonard, with his 'refreshing purity' (Noble (ed.), *Recollections*, p. 155), seemed in some ways to remain 'the administrator of the Hambantota District in Ceylon' (Garnett, *Deceived with Kindness*, p. 109).

*Leonard Woolf and Virginia Stephen, 1912, at the time of their engagement. Leonard to Virginia 1913: 'Sometimes ... I've thought it may be a bad thing to love anyo as I love you' (Gordon, A Writer's Life, pp. 149–50).*

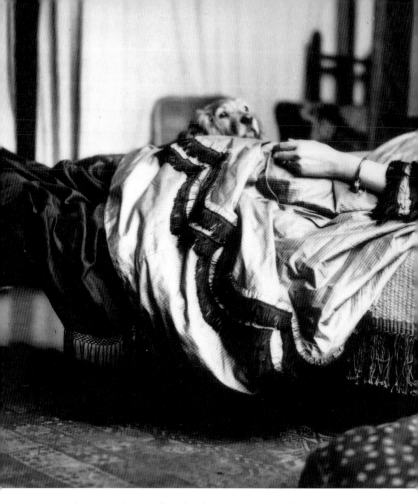

Couples, as we know, often develop their private fables. The Woolfs' version was set in the animal world, a world with which they were familiar. Virginia found this vocabulary and imagery reassuring for her emotional and sensual needs, a satisfactory substitute for other forms of personal involvement. She of course had been 'the Goat' in her family, and remained so to Vanessa. To Leonard, and then with intimate friends such as Vita Sackville-West,

*...mals, real and imagined, were a ...e part of Virginia's existence. She ...d herself 'Potto' and felt close to ...dogs: Pinker (Pinka) and Flush, ...ching over a resting Virginia.*

Virginia would sign herself Potto – a West African sloth, named after Bosman's *Guinea* (Lee, *Virginia Woolf*, p. 833), because of Virginia's lying on the sofa, an invalid. In her relation to Leonard, she would picture herself as a fierce West African baboon – Mandril Sarcophagus Felicissima va. Rarissima, rerum naturae simplex (al. Virginia Woolf) – who had in her service a Mongoose, whom she loved. 'The imposing creature then conceived a ridiculous passion for her unattractive servant with his thin, flea-ridden body' (Gordon, *A Writer's Life*, p. 142).

Everywhere they travelled, they were accompanied by Leonard's Mitz, his pet marmoset. He often judged the inhabitants of a country by their attitude towards Mitz, who was in any case an object of fascination. At home, their successive dogs took the place of the children Virginia was not allowed to have by the doctors who watched over her ceaselessly.

None of this fabled world of the Woolfs, of course, took the place of their serious commitment to a political stance, as important as their work. Leonard's Shavian leanings led him to a temporary involvement with Beatrice and Sidney Webb and the Fabian Society. Writing to Janet Case, her former Greek teacher, Virginia Woolf sums up a typical argument about George Bernard Shaw: 'I say the human heart is touched only by the poets. Leonard says rot, I say damn. Then we go home. Leonard says I'm narrow. I say he's stunted' (*Letters* 2, p. 529). They discussed, they argued, they worked together. Afterwards, he often wrote for the *New Statesman*, with a particular interest in the area of international governments, and their control, and taking part in the Executive Committee of the League of Nations. He was then the secretary to the Labour Party's Advisory Committee on International Questions. Virginia, who admired his political engagement, herself worked at the Women's Co-Operative Guild, a union of working-class women, and was involved in the Rodmell branch

*Overleaf  At Firle Park: Janet Case, Virginia Stephen and Vanessa Bell, 1911. Janet Case, trained in Classics at Cambridge, was Virginia's early teacher of Greek , and a lasting influence.*

*Portrait of Virginia Woolf by Duncan Grant. 'How I wish I wer a painter!' (Letters 6, p. 236).*

of the Labour Party. Leonard's *After the Deluge* concerned the possible forms of democratic government, and was published in the same month as *The Waves*, in October 1931, in the heated days of an election campaign about which his pessimism may have, it is speculated, had some basis in memories of ancestral oppression.

In Virginia's own most politicized text, *Three Guineas*, she made it clear just how outside convention and tradition she was choosing to be. Later, when public honours and titles were offered her, she would refuse them again on the grounds of her moral stance and status. Among her more noble honours was that of being the only woman ever to receive an invitation (in February 1932) to deliver the Clark Lectures at Cambridge. And yet she refused, realizing that to join even in that part of the university setting would be to forgo the status, no less treasured than crucial, of outsideness: 'My outsider's vision' (*Diary* 2, p. 55). Indeed, much of Bloomsbury's feeling of itself was that of opposition to the establishment, a kind of stubborn and joyous otherness.

Throughout her life, Virginia's otherness to institutions was opposed to, and in balance with, a closeness to her friends. In spite of her intense working passions, she made a deliberate effort to stay close to all of these, not only by seeing them but in particular by her correspondence, having an uncanny sense both of the persons to whom her missives were sent – and of the kind of value they (and she) placed on her way of recounting the simplest incidents. Her favourite thing was gossiping, with friends, with Leonard, but particularly with Vanessa. And, fortunately, their residences were no further apart than their feelings. Of the people in her life besides Leonard, Virginia Woolf remained closest to her sister Vanessa and her three children.

# Monk's House, Hogarth House and Charleston

*n-and-ink drawing of Virginia olf at the Hogarth Press. rting in April 1917, at Hogarth use, the Press occupied much of ginia's time: she placed the type, the text, did the binding and distributing.*

In January 1915, Virginia and Leonard found Hogarth House, at 17 Green, up the hill from Richmond High Street, which they leased. It also gave its name in 1917 to the Hogarth Press, which they ran for years, publishing, among many other important works, *The Waste Land* (1919) by T.S. Eliot (whom they would meet in 1918, when Eliot was still married to the highly strung Vivien Haigh-Wood and eager to publish his work with the Hogarth Press), Roger Fry's *The Artist and Psychoanalysis* (1924), James and Alix Strachey's translation of the works of Freud starting in 1924, and Gertrude Stein's *Composition as Explanation* (1926). Virginia would later describe the house to Jacques Raverat, in a letter of 1922, as 'rather nice, shabby, ancient, very solid & incredibly untidy' (*Letters* 2, p. 554). It was, in short, a grand place to work.

In May 1916, when he was bicycling in East Sussex, only four miles from Asheham, just below Firle Beacon, Leonard came across an unoccupied farmhouse, on the property of Lord Gage, who was delighted to rent it to the Bells. This was, of course, to be Charleston, into which Vanessa moved with Clive, who was involved from 1917 to 1923 with the elegant and tasteful Mary Hutchinson – what the French call a *jolie laide* or lovely-ugly woman – since Vanessa was now with Duncan Grant, who would become her lifelong companion. Duncan did the major part of the decorations at Charleston, and was, along with Vanessa, the spirit of the farmhouse but, given his propensities and, in particular, his relation with David (Bunny) Garnett, Vanessa's inner state was often one of distress. During the war, Duncan and Bunny did their wartime service at Wissett farm in Suffolk, as day labourers,

**Above** *Asheham House, 1914, with Leonard Woolf. Before they found nearby Monk's House and Charleston, Virginia Woolf and Vanessa Bell rented Asheham House, described by Leonard as 'romantic, gentle, melancholy, lovely' (Beginning Again, p. 67).*

**Left** *Lytton Strachey, Duncan Grant, Clive Bell, at Asheham, Sussex, 19. Asheham preceded both Monk's House and Charleston as the gathering place for the Bloomsbury group. In an illicit gathering, Dora Carrington and others broke in one night to sleep, later apologizing.*

**ht** *Vanessa Bell*, The Tub, *1917.*
*essa Bell's disturbing painting*
*he upended Omega-shaped tub*
*inally pictured Mary Hutchinson*
*er husband Clive's mistress – in*
*nightdress. The three flowers*
*e been interpreted as reflecting*
*situation of Duncan Grant, his*
*er David Garnett, and Vanessa,*
*ove with Duncan. It relates to*
*ious bath paintings by Edgar*
*gas, so admired by Vanessa,*
*to those by Duncan himself.*

essential to supply food for the war effort. They remained close to Charleston, whose house, garden and spirit continue to this day.

When, in order to make Bunny jealous, as the story goes, Duncan took Vanessa to bed, he left his diary open at the relevant page: 'That's one for you, Bunny!' The result was the birth of Angelica, on Christmas Day 1918; Bunny announced that he would marry the little girl when she grew up. She was given the name of Bell, as if she had been Clive's, like her brothers Julian and Quentin. Angelica and Bunny were to begin an affair in 1938, to the distress of both Duncan and Vanessa, and eventually married, just as Bunny had predicted, and had four daughters. Angelica's moving volume of 1984, *Deceived with Kindness*, tells the story.

To Vanessa's boys, Julian and Quentin (originally Claudian Stephen, to which Quentin was added), Virginia felt very close. She had tried to have them stay with her during the time of Angelica's birth in 1918, but the experience had not been wildly successful, since she tired far too easily. Perhaps the doctors who had advised

**Left** *Quentin and Julian Bell, Vanessa's children by Clive Bell. Virginia Woolf had tried to have h nephews, whom she greatly loved, stay with her during the time of Angelica's birth in 1918, but the experience had not been wildly successful, since she tired far too easily.*

against her ever having children were right. She had always envied Vanessa for her original earthiness and her evident *joie de vivre*: Duncan and Vanessa seemed to be, as she put it, 'humming with heat and happiness' (*Letters* 3, p. 203). Their passion for painting overcame whatever temporary irritations there might have been, along with their happiness at being together.

Charleston itself was, by all accounts, not only a centre of astounding creativity – the painters always painting, the writers always writing, everyone always doing something – but, at that round table in the dining room, the conversation was always stimulating, particularly when Roger Fry was around. Virginia tells of one such occasion, and it could stand for them all: 'We discuss prose; and as usual some book is had out, and I have to read a passage over his shoulder. Theories are fabricated. Pictures stood on chairs' (*Diary* 1, pp. 140, 141).

*ove  Vanessa Bell painting at
arleston, 1936. More than any-
ng, Vanessa loved painting –
did Duncan Grant. For years
d years, they lived and worked
ether. This is one of Duncan's
ny tributes to her and her work.*

*ow  Duncan Grant, Angelica Bell,
ger Fry at Charleston. Angelica
h her father and Charleston's
ourite visitor: everything seemed
re lively when Roger was around,
e was always to say (conversation
h the author).*

*John Maynard Keynes and Duncan Grant, 1912. Early on, Duncan was Keynes's lover after a close involvement with his cousin, Lytton Strachey, who wrote him on 6 October 1905: 'Beloved, do you know how happy it makes me to think that you love me?' Keynes had his own room at Charleston, where he wrote his celebrated* Economic Consequences of the Peace.

*ove* Cézanne's Apples. *This
*inting, purchased from the Degas
*e in Paris, was left, famously, by
*n Maynard Keynes in a hedge
*side Charleston Farmhouse as a
*prise, and then brought in and
*cussed at length. 'We discuss
*se; and as usual some book is
*d out, and I have to read a pas-
*e over his shoulder. Theories are
*ricated. Pictures stood on chairs'
*ary 1, pp. 140, 141).*

In 1919, when the owner of Asheham needed it for his own use, Virginia found an old windmill in the centre of Lewes, not far from Asheham, in East Sussex. She took Leonard to see it – he found it too small. But two miles from Lewes, and on the other side of the Ouse, they passed a notice about Monk's House in Rodmell. They bid for it at auction, and made it their home on long weekends and for two months in the summer. Virginia loved to stride across the very English landscape of the nearby Sussex Downs. For her, the countryside around her house and the view of the Downs (*Diary* 2, p. 50) found 'all the elements of the English brought together accidentally'. 'Monk's House,' she said in her happiness with it, 'will be our address for ever and ever' (Lee, *Virginia Woolf*, p. 421). She had even marked the place for their graves there, near their meadow.

In Monk's House, she had a writing studio in the garden, and

*ove  Vanessa's paintings of the*
*thouse at Godrevy on the tiles*
*the fireplace in Virginia's garden*
*m at Monk's House.*

*ft  Monk's House, in Rodmell,*
*ar Lewes and Charleston, repre-*
*ted Englishness for Virginia:*
*ur address forever ...'*

Leonard, after having contemplated building a greenhouse nearby that would have cut off her view, finally placed a modified version behind the house. Upstairs, above the dining room, was a room with two large windows, where most of the portraits of Virginia after 1919 are taken. She had written reviews, as she would her entire life long, and *The Voyage Out* (haunted by her early child-hood experience with sexual threat), and had start-ed *Night and Day*. With her proceeds from *Mrs Dalloway*, the first of her novels to become a financial success, she had arranged a bath-tub in which she would declaim in the morning the sentences she had written the day before, to get the proper resonance. In her gar-den room, the tiles on the fireplace were Vanessa's paintings of the lighthouse at Godrevy, lest Virginia forget, as she never would, the family summers at St Ives. So Charleston was, along with Monk's

House, and those few squares and streets of London, the heart of ongoing Bloomsbury.

Monk's House was a perfect place for living and for visitors, for Leonard's gardening and their writing. Endless discussions took place there, some of which are recounted in Virginia's letters. Work went on constantly wherever Virginia and Leonard were, whether in Hogarth House or Monk's House. Many of their friends they met through their publishing venture. One of these was T. S. Eliot – Eliot's great *Waste Land* was the cornerstone of their modernist publishing, and his submission of it was their introduction to him. He became increasingly a close friend, after an initial hesitation. 'We've been having that strange young man Eliot to dinner. His sentences take such an enormous time to spread themselves out that we didn't get very far; but we did reach Ezra Pound and Wyndham Lewis and

**Above** *Leonard Woolf's study at Monk's House. 'Are you in your study, brother? … Well, what can trouble this happiness?'* (Diary 6, p. 520).

**Right** *Virginia Woolf at Monk's House with John Lehmann. John worked with Leonard and Virginia at the Hogarth Press, thought its decisions 'revolutionary', and was a major influence on its poetry list in the 1930s.*

ginia Woolf, Charles Mauron and 'en Anrep bowling at Monk's use, August 1937. In her diary that month and year, Virginia tes, 'Eddie Playfair and the urons impend ... bowls have ome a passion. I gave up a walk lay.'

how they were great geniuses, and Mr. James Joyce, which I'm more prepared to agree to, but why has Eliot stuck in this mud? Can't his culture carry him through, or does culture land one there?' (*Letters* 2, p. 296).

As Virginia writes to Roger Fry, Eliot aroused her constant fascination – but somehow always associated with a certain distrust, because of his, and thus his interlocutor's, never being sure of exactly what he meant. For someone so delicately balanced between clarity and a highly strung lyric sensitivity as Virginia, this was at once mystifying and magnetizing. Eliot always struck her as remarkable, in such conflict with all the many forces inside and against him: 'The wild eye still; but all rocky, yellow, driven, & constricted. Sits very solid – large shoulders – in his chair ... But to me, still, a dear old ass. I mean I cant be frozen off with this divine authority any longer.' She could not bear, she said, the penitential ash-bin she felt the audience for Eliot's *Murder in the Cathedral* was forced to roll in, calling him, in no uncertain terms, an American eunuch (*Letters* 5, p. 448). This is an interesting point to meditate, given the general impression of the mentally sick Virginia Woolf: she was, in fact, very much on the positive, even ecstatic, side of life, and fundamentally opposed, as she phrased it to her nephew Julian Bell, who was teaching in Wuhan University in China, to the 'general worship of decay and the skeleton'. With her strongly anti-religious bent, Virginia was unlikely to share the viewpoint of the Eliot who had converted to the High Anglican Church. Perhaps this conversion was partly responsible for what she came to consider his 'eel-like' self, whom she pictured slithering this way and that, not as solid as he had seemed initially, with his broad shoulders.

When, in 1920, Pound started the 'Bel Esprit' fund to get Eliot out of the bank where he worked, in order to write his poetry, Eliot's reaction bothered Virginia as to her friends. His 'peevish, plaintive, egotistical' indecision (Lee, *Virginia Woolf*, p. 446) was intensely irritating, as was his reprinting of *The Waste Land* in his collected *Poems 1909–1925* with Faber and Faber, the rivals of the Hogarth

*Left* T. S. Eliot, Virginia Woolf an
Vivien Eliot, 1932. 'Tom' Eliot, the
'American eunuch', and Virginia
were close friends over the years.
He frequently visited Monk's
House, and had come here with
his unstable first wife. 'The wild e
still; but all rocky, yellow, driven,
& constricted.'

Press, without giving them any warning. 'Tom has treated us scurvi-
ly ... ' (*Diary* 3, p. 41). He came visiting once with his wife Vivien, in
her white taffeta dress and handkerchief soaked in ether – presum-
ably against fainting fits. She was a paranoid case, suffering frequent delusions, and Eliot finally divorced her. His relations with
Virginia were not without complications, as one would expect of
two such writers.

# Auppegard, Roquebrune and Cassis

Since the distance to France from England was so slight, all the Bloomsberries went over to the Continent quite often, generally spending two or three weeks there in the spring. Virginia had first gone over with Vanessa early on, after the death of their father in 1904, and later, in 1907, had gone with her brother Adrian, Leonard, Vanessa and Clive to Paris. Vanessa was always to spend a good deal of time in Paris, far more than Virginia, for it was a perfect

*ht The painter Ethel Sands at Château d'Auppegard before the co on the loggia she had com-sioned from Vanessa Bell and ncan Grant in 1927. Ethel started lon in her Chelsea home, 15 The e, in March 1923, of which Lytton chey attended the opening.*

**Above left**  The French painter
Simon Bussy was a great friend of
Henri Matisse, with whom he had
studied under Gustave Moreau.
He had met Lytton Strachey's sister
Dorothy when he came to study in
England.

*above André Gide and Dorothy
Strachey Bussy at breakfast at
Pontigny, for a 'Décade' during
10-22 August 1922. (The Virginia
Woolf 'décade' was held at Cerisy,
the successor to Pontigny; in July
2001, there was another.) It was
after the Pontigny breakfast that
André Gide informed Dorothy
Strachey that he was the father-to-
be of a child who was Catherine
Gide, daughter of Elizabeth von
Asselberghe, who had been in love
with Rupert Brooke before he went
to the war.*

place to paint, to keep up with what was being
exhibited, and with other painters. Clive was
almost a Parisian, and circulated freely among the
artists there, as did Roger Fry. Vanessa and Clive's
boys Quentin and Julian were at school near
Paris, while their younger sister Angelica was with
Vanessa and Duncan.

Vanessa and Duncan, and/or Leonard and
Virginia, would generally take the ferry from
Newhaven to Dieppe, and spend the night with
the painters Ethel Sands and Nan Hudson at
Auppegard, just outside Dieppe. Their way of living was one of absolute neatness and formality,
the model, thought Virginia, of a lesbian house-
hold. The partners were very different, as she
recounts one of their visits. '"I'm gregarious," said Ethel a little
waspishly, for she is brittle & acid, the spoilt pet of the more dour
& upstanding Nan. We were, I think looking over the cliff with the
churchyard on it, the tombstones standing up against the blue sea'

(*Diary* 2, p. 158). The loggia of this house was painted, in cheerful harvest decoration, by Vanessa and Duncan in 1927.

The Woolfs travelled all over France, in Normandy and Burgundy, with Virginia making extensive notations on her observations. One of the more important places they visited in the south of France, or the Midi, was the home of the Bussys at Roquebrune, near Menton

*mon Bussy, portrait of Lytton
achey in 1904, painted at La
uco. Every detail, from the crossed
s and delicate slippers to the
y he holds the pen, captures
ssy's brother-in-law's meticulous
gance.*

on the Riviera. Simon Bussy, the short French painter from Dole and a friend of Lytton Strachey, had come to England to study and had married Dorothy, one of Lytton's many sisters and the translator of Gide. She was the author of the anonymously signed *Olivia*, a tale of subtly stated lesbian love based on the girls' school called Les Ruches, outside Fontainebleau, and run by Madame Souvestre, a close friend of Lady Strachey, and attended by Eleanor Roosevelt and other equally celebrated women. Gide took fourteen years to read it, and when it was finally published to great acclaim, Dorothy teased him about his having turned down Proust's long novel for Gallimard, and her far shorter one. He wired back that these were the worst two judgements he had ever made. But his support of Simon Bussy was constant, arranging exhibitions for him, and speaking highly of his work whenever he could.

Simon Bussy's portraits of his brother-in-law, Lytton, of Maynard Keynes, of Ottoline Morrell with green hair, and of Dorothy are outstanding. More surprising are his detailed paintings of animals: when Dorothy would spend time with Gide or in galleries, he would spend his in the zoo. Angelica Garnett, speaking of the pairs of animals Bussy often painted, in his longing for symmetry, speaks of the compelling 'precision, delicacy and brilliance' of his animal paintings (Garnett, *The Eternal Moment*, p. 97). The painter Dunoyer de Segonzac admired the 'grandeur in their restrained dimensions'. (Caws, *Bloomsbury and France*, p. 333) The Bussys came over yearly to England, and were close to the Bloomsbury group, their daughter Janie being a frequent visitor to Charleston. Their house, La Souco, was a welcoming point for Lytton and the others.

Vanessa painted often at La Souco, once capturing, in yellows and greens like a garden in sunlight, the figure of the elderly Dorothy walking in from the courtyard, and was herself painted by Duncan as she painted there. During the war, the Bussys rented their house to André Malraux, and themselves stayed in Nice, next to Henri Matisse, whom Simon had known in their classes at the

46    Virginia Woolf

Dorothy Bussy in chair with
picture book, Janie Bussy behind
chair, 1937. Dorothy Strachey Bussy,
André Gide's translator, and author
the brief novel Olivia, published
pseudonymously, about Madame
Sylvestre's school in Fontainebleau.

**Below** Vanessa Bell, Dorothy
Bussy at La Souco, 1954. La Souco,
in the Mediterranean village of
Roquebrune, was the home of
Simon Bussy, a French painter, and
his wife Dorothy Strachey Bussy,
one of Lytton Strachey's sisters.

Beaux-Arts with Gustave Moreau. Matisse relied on Simon for his counsel, and on the family for a listening ear and daily tea, occasioning Janie Bussy's delightfully wicked account of his arrogance: He wakes every morning and gives thanks to God, she said, for being Henri Matisse.

*Left* Vanessa Bell Painting at La Souco. *The painter Duncan Grant renders a perfect tribute to Vanessa who always loved him, hard at work at the Bussys' home at Roquebrune, one shoe dangling.*

The Woolfs would travel around, often visiting the Raverats in Vence. Virginia had had a brief flirtation with Jacques, who had married Gwen Darwin, a writer and painter, the granddaughter of Charles Darwin. Gwen had previously been involved with another

*Left* Jacques Raverat, French
painter, lived with his wife Gwen
Darwin in Vence. He maintained
extensive correspondence with
Virginia, who found him 'so clear
and logical and intense'.
Increasingly paralysed, he died
early from multiple sclerosis.

*Right* Gwen Darwin Raverat,
English painter, photograph by
Sophie Gurney. Virginia and Gwen
had been friends at Cambridge,
where Gwen had been in love with
Rupert Brooke.

of Virginia's friends, the glamorous Rupert Brooke,
and the group Virginia called Neo-Pagans, for
their wandering about barefoot and frequently
unclothed in the woods around Cambridge.
Virginia's letters to Jacques, and his to her, are
of particular interest as they tackle all manner of
philosophical subjects, from religion to homosexu-
ality. Jacques remained in particular need of her
letters, for he suffered progressively from dissemi-
nated sclerosis, and died an early death in 1925.

Most important of all were the visits of Leonard
and Virginia to Cassis, a small fishing village
southeast of Marseilles in the French Midi.
Duncan Grant's aunt, Daisy McNeil, lived there,
in Les Mimosas, a house she rented from the
English painter, writer, and surrealist Roland Penrose. Her skiff, the
*Arequipa*, anchored in the harbour, was the setting for many rowdy
parties. Duncan and Vanessa visited her, staying in a rented house,
then found their own place, La Bergère, on the winegrowing estate

**Left** Duncan Grant and Vanessa Bell at La Bergère, photograph by Lytton Strachey, 1928. 'Completely absolutely and eternally happy' in Cassis (Letters 3, p. 452).

**Right** Fontcreuse, 1990. The home of Peter Teed and Jean Campbell, where the Woolfs often visited. Leonard of Peter: 'Beneath the immaculate surface of the colonel of a crack regiment Teed was fundamentally an intellectual who liked artists and intellectuals' (Downhill, p. 181).

*Peter Teed and Jean Campbell*
*[F]ontcreuse, 1928. This couple*
*[ar]e immensely fond of Vanessa*
*[&] Duncan, and of Virginia and*
*[Leo]nard also. At Peter's death,*
*[Jero]me Hill, founder of the Camargo*
*[Fou]ndation, arranged to have*
*[the] furniture from Fontcreuse sold*
*[to m]ake Jean's last days more*
*[com]fortable.*

*[bel]ow La Bergère, Cassis, 1990.*
*[Th]e house is on the property of*
*[Fon]tcreuse, rented by Vanessa,*
*[Dun]can and Clive in 1927 and 1928.*
*['Th]e light & sun are even now aston-*
*[ishi]ng after London,' Vanessa writes*
*[Vir]ginia (Letters, 26 January 1927).*

of Fontcreuse just outside Cassis. They located it in 1927 through Penrose, a close friend of Picasso and of Roger Fry. Colonel Teed, retired from service in India, and his companion Jean Campbell, owned the estate and a great vineyard, where they all had their first (and only) acquaintance with the harvest of grapes. The celebrated white wine of Cassis, among whose labels that of Fontcreuse is still outstanding, was a delight to Virginia, who pictured herself and Leonard settling down gloriously near Vanessa, living on olives and wine, and writing and painting: Bloomsbury on the Mediterranean, as they all thought of it there, as long as it lasted.

Cassis was a traditional haunt of French painters, such as Derain and Matisse, and it was still now full of English painters, a society which Duncan and Vanessa fled, preferring to paint on their own, and live their quiet life. Virginia and Leonard first visited Vanessa and Duncan in Cassis in the spring of 1925, after leaving Newhaven and going to Troyes, Beaune, Vienne, Orange, Aix, and finally Cassis. Virginia and

Cassis, photograph by Lytton Strachey. 'Absolute heaven, I think it. Everything looks odd and new …' (Virginia to Gwen Raverat, Letters, 3, p. 483).

Leonard would stay at Fontcreuse, as she wrote to Margaret Llewellyn Davies (*Letters* 4, p. 65): 'Nessa's villa is five minutes off, and L. and I live up here, on a verandah, and go to her for meals – a delicious life, with a great deal of wine, cheap cigars, conversation.' Not that there was not conversation everywhere Virginia was, but that, here in the Midi, it seemed particularly nourished by the atmosphere. Virginia wrote to her sister of her desire to live at least '2 months in France and see the anenomes open and hear some 24 nightingales and go gliding in and out of the bays' (*Letters* 4, p. 120). She would walk to nearby La Ciotat, noting the red tulips scattered over the fields with their rows of vines and an occasional fruit tree. She noted everything, with the same definite clarity she found in the landscape:

> *Here & there was an angular white, or yellow or blue washed house, with all its shutters tightly closed; & flat paths round it & once rows of stocks; an incomparable cleanness & definiteness every where. All these bays are very circular, & fringed with the pale coloured plaster houses, very tall, shutters, patched & peeled, now with a pot & tufts of green on them, now with clothes drying; an old woman looking* (Diary 3, p. 8).

The heat and light of Southern France, contrasted with the gloom of England, brought out in her a special joy: 'Nobody shall say of me that I have not known perfect happiness, but few could put their finger on the moment, or say what made it' (*Diary* 3, p. 9). Nor could she, except that whatever intensity of atmosphere enabled it, she was always on the alert to spot it and record it.

*Duncan Grant sketching at Bergère, Cassis, 1928. Duncan is acknowledged as a successful painter throughout his long life: Cassis supplied one of his most colourful motifs, exemplified in his Window, South of France, from the same year.*

In 1927 and 1928, Vanessa and Duncan spent several months in Cassis, their painting profiting from the Mediterranean light and brilliance of living. When, in 1929, Virginia had her fantasy of settling near Vanessa and Duncan in La Boudarde, a simple three-room 'hut' they saw, in the forest near Fontcreuse, and that she and Leonard had thought of buying, Leonard was not keen on the idea. They actually shipped furniture over from England, had windows put in, and bought sheets for it, but then went no further. They gave the furniture and sheets to Jean Campbell at Fontcreuse and gave up the plan. It might well never have worked out in any case, given her lack of proficiency in French, in spite of the lessons she took with Janie Bussy. She could read it perfectly, but her unease with the spoken tongue would have

proved impracticable, particularly for a person so in love with language.

Yet her love affair with Cassis definitely nourished her fiction: *The Waves*, perhaps her greatest triumph of lyric writing, was originally called 'The Moths', based on Vanessa's experience of them in the Midi, where they would fly at night towards the light, in the open window of

*Above* Duncan Grant, Window, South of France, *1928. This windo is at La Bergère, the house Vaness and Duncan rented, looking out c the Fontcreuse vineyard.*

*ow* Angelica Bell in an olive tree, *...ssis*, 1927. *This was the first year ...essa and Duncan had rented ...Bergère.*

La Bergère. That novel, really a long prose poem that Virginia called her 'eyeless book', turns around a group of six children growing up, their reactions intertwined with the daily cycles of nature, and then, later, around a missing centre: Perceval, based on Thoby Stephen. He is pictured (ironically or not) as a glorious warrior. After reading it, Vanessa wrote to her sister (*Letters* 4, p. 390): 'I think you have made one's human feelings into something less personal – if you wouldn't think me foolish, I should say you have found the "lulla-by capable of singing him to rest".'

*ginia Woolf, Angelica Bell, *nard Woolf, Judith Bagenal, *La Bergère, Cassis, 1929. Judith, * daughter of Barbara Bagenal *le 'Babs', Clive Bell's friend), *s a friend of Angelica. Virginia of *ssis: 'But this is all I want; I could * think of anything better' (Diary *. 9). But as Angela Garnett *lains: 'Because Leonard wasn't *keen on going abroad, whatever *ginia felt about it ...' (conversa-*n, 1990).

# Virginia and Vita

Virginia's intimacy with Vita Sackville-West, whose long aristocratic lineage and easy opulent manner was eventually of great appeal, did not begin immediately begin when they met in 1922, when Vita was introduced by Clive into the group. That 'florid, moustached, parakeet coloured ... hard handsome' apparition was not such as to inspire instant devotion. Virginia found Vita lacking in wit, as she was to find her alway busy pen 'of brass' when compared with the great attraction of her long stride across her ancestral fields, accompanied by her

*Below* Vita Sackville-West in chair at Monk's House. Virginia to Vita. 'I suppose your orchard is beginning to dapple as it did the day I came there. One of the sights I shall see my death bed' (Letters 11, p. 476)

*above Vita Sackville-West, 1925, with her beloved Sarah. Vita writes her husband Harold Nicolson: 'I the Mrs. Woolf with a sick passion.'*

many dogs. That Vita should have appeared just after the death of Katherine Mansfield, to whom Virginia's attraction was of a constant ambivalence, is not unimportant.

Vita's tendencies were mainly lesbian, yet she had a wonderfully successful marriage to the diplomat Harold Nicolson, himself homosexual. Vita, involved throughout her life with a long list of

*Left* Vita Sackville-West and Virginia Woolf. The two writers were great friends, before, during, and after Virginia's tribute to Vita, Orlando.

*Right* Vita Sackville-West in France, photograph by Virginia Woolf; or Virginia photographed by Vita: probably the former, although no one seems certain. Their celebrated trip in 1928 through Burgundy lasted five days: they spent much of their time concerned over mail from the husbands.

women lovers, had had one flagrant, famous, and lengthy affair with Violet Keppel, the daughter of King Edward VII's mistress. After Violet married Denys Trefusis, in despair over Vita's infidelity to her, they 'eloped' to France in 1918, Violet as Eve and Vita as a dashing, romantically clothed gentleman called Julian. The affair is recounted, lightly disguised, in their joint novel, *Challenge*. This escapade occasioned a rescue by both husbands, who took an airplane over to bring back their errant spouses.

The mutual attraction between Vita Sackville-West and Virginia Woolf dates from the end of 1922. As Vita wrote to her closest friend, and husband, Harold Nicolson: 'I love Mrs. Woolf with a sick passion.' But she was always – with reason, of course – afraid

of Virginia's fragility of body and mind, and so treated her different-
ly from her other lovers. On her side, Virginia found in Vita, of
whom the Bloomsbury group continued to make fun for her slow-
ness, something 'dense instead of vibrant', calling her with affection but also with a certain tinge of condescension 'donkey West'.
In spite of her own more than affectionate feelings for Vita, she
feared, rightly, that Vita and her diplomat husband would not be
able to fit in at 46 Gordon Square with the others: Vanessa, Clive,
Duncan, Leonard, and the highly judgemental Lytton. 'We judged
them both incurably stupid,' she finally says. All they lack is 'what
we have – some cutting edge, some invaluable idiosyncrasy, intensity, for which I would not have all the sons & all the moons in
the world' (*Diary* 3, p. 146). And Vita, in her turn, judged the life
at Charleston Farmhouse to be 'very plain living and high thinking',
as she wrote to Harold.

Despite Virginia's appraisal of Vita's brains, she was attracted,
in Vita, to her aristocratic heritage, to her ancestral homes at Knole
and Long Barn. When she was first invited by Vita to visit Long
Barn, in the car was one of Vita's lesbian lovers, Dorothy Wellesley,
and the writer Geoffrey Scott – eight years older than Vita and wed-
ded to the still older Lady Sybil Cutting. They were both in love with
Vita. In her turn, Virginia was smitten, if temporarily (long enough,
thank goodness, to write the history of the androgynous and beautiful *Orlando*), by her background, her easy bearing, and her appearance: 'All these ancestors & centuries, & silver & gold, have bred
a perfect body' (Lee, *Virginia Woolf*, p. 495). Vita was an easy and
opulent mass of contradictions, living a life of great indulgence,
full of books and biscuits, of Persian rugs and dogs, log fires, and
butlers, with 'manly good sense and simplicity ... O yes, I like her;
could tack her on to my equipage for all time ...' (*Diary* 2, p. 313).
In her brown velvet coat, its pockets always baggy, and her long
pearl necklace, she was very 'free & easy, always giving me great
pleasure to watch, & recalling some image of a ship breasting a
sea, nobly, magnificently, with all sails spread, & the gold sunlight
on them' (*Diary* 3, p. 146).

Vita's most interesting novel – really a long tale – *Seducers in*

Above Photo by Leonard Woolf of Virginia Woolf and Vita Sackville-West in 1932. Virginia to Vita, 8 April 1926: '… one of the reasons that I like women better (even platonically) is that they take more trouble and are more skilled in the art of making friendships into a shape.'

Below Photo by Leonard Woolf of Vita Sackville-West, Virginia Woolf and dogs on the same hill on the same day in 1932. 'And I don't lose any of my liking for her gentleness, faithfulness, modesty' (Diary 5, 149). 'But I love you, Virginia – there. Are you pleased?' (Vita to Virginia, 30 March 1928).

*Ecuador*, in 1923, about the way in which the tint of one's glasses can transform one's vision and one's life, was dedicated to Virginia Woolf, who preferred it to any of Vita's other writings. On Vita's writing desk, she kept a photograph of Virginia, and they remained friends, even though Vita had many other lovers, about whom Virginia would tease her: you love them more carnally, and so on. Writing to Vita on 18 March 1933 (*Letters* 5, p. 170),

*Vita Sackville-West on mule from Twelve Days in the Bakhtian Mountains (1927). Vita was a gre traveller, in Persia, in Russia, and even in the United States. '... als I want nine lives at least ... and*

she pleads with her: either she comes, preferably with Sarah her dog, or she and Leonard will dash off to Italy to try out their new car with its fly wheel on the Alps! 'Please Vita darling come back soon ... Please come snuffing up my stairs soon, just the same, in your red jersey. Please wear your pearls. Please bring Sarah.'

When Harold was posted to Tehran, in September 1925, and Vita was to join him in the

more planets to explore' (Vita to Virginia, 8 February 1926). 'Why weren't you there?' (Vita to Virginia, 9 March 1926). 'Please miss me' 10 March 1927).

New Year, Virginia was feeling lonesome. So Leonard urged her to invite herself to Long Barn, which she did. To Vita's delight, Virginia greatly liked the long poem 'The Land'. That night, she and Vita stayed up and talked, and finally made love, which they did, according to Vita's correspondence with Harold, exactly twice. In Vita's diary entry for one of these dates, the day is simply marked with a very large X (Lilly Library, unpublished). When Vita wrote to Harold about their affair, Harold reminded her that she did not have '*la main heureuse*', or a nourishing influence on married couples (Lee, *Virginia Woolf*, p. 499). In fact, he was right. Several of her women lovers had left their husbands for her, and Geoffrey Scott's marriage broke up over her but she never left Harold.

Virginia's descriptions of Vita are the best we have, even before she set to writing that long love letter to Vita, called *Orlando*: the story of an aristocratic young man who becomes a lovely young woman. Much about Vita and about their relation had to do with a fluid freedom. For, of course, Vita was not simply a Sapphist, rather, and more interestingly, one of those women who, in Virginia's own books, 'moved fluidly between the roles of mothers and daughters, sisters and friends' (Lee, *Virginia Woolf*, p. 491). This was no doubt Virginia's central relationship in her forties, after which, in the 1930s, she was gradually disenchanted because of Vita's heavy drinking and increasingly manly appearance. Nevertheless, their closeness endured until Virginia's end: 'You have given me such happiness,' she writes in 1940 (*Letters* 4, p. 13).

# Travelling with Leonard and also with Roger

Leonard and Virginia loved to drive around on their travels. They exchanged their Singer car, purchased in 1928 and affectionately known as 'The Umbrella' (with which they had toured France so often, and gone down to Cassis to visit Vanessa and Duncan), for a Lanchester in January 1933. They often drove in this grand vehicle, with its handsome green enamelled body and silver convertible top, taking it across on the ferry from England. They went to Ireland, spending time in Galway and admiring the Cliffs of Moher – those extraordinary protruberances jutting out into the blue sea. In 1938, they went to Scotland and the Isle of Skye, admiring everywhere the austere beauty of the highlands, the brooding clouds, and the dark lakes, of which Leonard took many pictures, and marvelling at the famous breakfasts. They elicited Virginia's irony: as she wrote to Vanessa: 'And the porridge is a dream. Only I loathe porridge' (*Letters* 6, p. 249). Everywhere, of course, they took Mitz.

One of Virginia's most notable trips without Leonard was in 1932, to Greece, when she accompanied Roger Fry and his sister Margery, the principal of Somerville College in Oxford, no less learned and energetic than her brother. Virginia always found Roger better to travel with than anyone, for his curiosity, tirelessness and seemingly endless knowledge. They were in Athens on 20 April, toured through the Peloponnese on 25–28 April, and went to Delphi from 30 April through to 2 May. Of all the many images Virginia retained of this trip – some captured in her photographs, of Roger on his mule, of Roger sketching, and Margery's picture of Roger and Virginia, laughing together – she was particularly struck by the Parthenon, this image with its marble columns at the world's end.

What amazing endurers that brother and sister were, as she

wrote to Quentin that May. Even with the pain Roger must have suffered with his piles, nothing would stop him or his sister. They kept up a constant supply of talk about everything they saw and knew. Both brother and sister were erudite beyond belief: if the slightest flower escaped him, it would not elude Margery. They identified every 'bird, beast and stone. Even when Roger's inside is falling down, and Margery must make water instantly or perish, one has only to mention Themistocles and the battle of Platea for them both to become like youth at its spring' (*Letters* 5, p. 56).

Roger was in constant admiration of both art and life, as Virginia wrote in her diary during the entire trip. He would exclaim over and over, excited as he was always by art and by much else – he was one of the world's great enthusiasts – 'oh come and look at this! My word that's swell – very swell' (*Letters* 5, p. 59). He would exclaim, put down his hat, stick, his guides and dictionaries, and go peer at whatever marvel he detected. His energy was mind-boggling, on this trip and on every other: from early to late, he would lead his friends to churches far out of the way, to small and unknown restaurants, on expeditions far and wide and particularly long. Exhausted, his companions would plead that it was lunchtime. There was always just one more thing to see, for hours to come. He was an endless fountain of knowledge, and that very endlessness wore out the others. Clive, who was rather inclined to mock him, would describe how late at night – after poring over the translation of yet one more Mallarmé sonnet with Julian – Roger would plead for another chess game just before midnight and then himself stay up reading Greek. Virginia loved this in him, and admired him all her life.

Roger always knew how to see, to show and to remain silent. Virginia's description of one of his celebrated lectures in the Queen's Hall recounts it best. The immense audience that thronged to hear him included many painters: Walter Sickert

*ginia Woolf and Roger Fry in*
*ece, 1932. Virginia notes in her*
*ry, after writing Roger's biogra-*
*: 'What a curious relation is*
*ne with Roger at this moment*
*vho have given him a kind of*
*pe after his death – was he like*
*t?' (Diary 5, p. 305). Virginia*
*Ethel Smyth, 11 September 1934:*
*e most heavenly of men ... so*
*, so infinitely gifted' (Letters 5,*
*30).*

*4  Photograph by Virginia Woolf*
*Roger Fry reading on mule in*
*…ece, 1932. 'Dignified ₰ honest ₰*
*…ge – "large sweet soul" – some-*
*…ng ripe ₰ musical about him – ₰*
*…n the fun ₰ the fact that he had*
*…d with such generosity ₰ curiosi-*
*…(Diary 4, p. 243).*

*…ht  Walter Sickert, caricature of*
*…ger Fry lecturing, 1911. Virginia of*
*…ger: 'He was always the giver –*
*…one excited and stirred me as he*
*…' (Fry, Letters 1, p. 95). Aldous*
*…xley: 'Old Roger Fry, who for a*
*…n of over fifty is far the youngest*
*…son I have ever seen' (Fry, Letters*
*…. 59).*

'VISION  VOLUMES  AND  RECESSION

described how he would rush, like a sheep, to the feet of this shep-
herd. Even Carrington, whose work Roger Fry had not always cham-
pioned, would go and listen with enthusiasm. For he had, better
than any other lecturer, the gift of making others see. Somehow,
as Virginia told it, the black and white slide on the screen became
radiant through the mist, and took on the grain and texture of the
actual canvas … 'and finally the lecturer, after looking long through
his spectacles, came to a pause. He was pointing to the late work
by Cézanne, and he was baffled. He shook his head; his stick rested
on the floor. It went, he said, far beyond any analysis of which he
was capable. And so instead of saying, "Next slide", he bowed, and

MANET
CEZANNE
GAUGUIN
VANGOGH
MATISSE
&
NOV· 8
TO
JAN· 15·

GRAFTON·GALLERY
MANET AND THE
POST·IMPRESSIONISTS

*Poster: Grafton Gallery: Manet and the Post-Impressionists: Manet, Cézanne, Gauguin, Van Gogh, Matisse, etc. Roger Fry's much celebrated and much reviled 1910 exhibition that brought French art to English artists, and may have occasioned Virginia Woolf's frequently quoted remark: 'On or about December 1910 human character changed.'*

the audience emptied itself into Langham Place' (*Roger Fry*, p. 263). She most admired his endless and informed enthusiasm, the way in which his mind was, as she wrote to her friend, the elderly composer Ethyl Smyth, 'so rich so infinitely gifted – and oh how we've talked and talked – for 20 years now' (*Letters* 5, p. 330).

Fry was responsible for the ultra-famous Manet and the Post-Impressionists Exhibition at the Grafton Galleries in London, from 8 November 1909 to 15 January 1910, in which French painters such as Cézanne, Gauguin, and Matisse were shown, and made an indelible impression on English art. Desmond McCarthy, who with his wife Mary was a close friend of the Bloomsberries, was responsible for the catalogue, which espoused Fry's enthusisam.

Of all the Bloomsbury group, Roger Fry is the person who elicited the greatest warmth of response from everyone I have ever spoken with, from Quentin Bell to Frances Partridge. He was, they all said, the most interesting and interested of anyone: to this Virginia was bound to respond. To his death from the consequences of a fall, in 1934, Virginia reacted strongly and in self-revelation. His funeral provoked in her first a fright, and then the full consciousness of her duty to herself as a writer: 'Of course I shall lie there too before the gate, & slide in; & it frightened me ... I felt the vainness of this perpetual fight, with our brains & loving each other against the other thing: if Roger could die ... ' and then came 'the exalted sense of being above time & death which comes from being again in a writing mood' (*Diary 4*, pp. 244–5). She reflected ironically that Roger, of all her friends, would best have understood the excitement she felt.

*low  Roger Fry with paintbox,
o. Roger always carried painting
terials with him, wherever he
nt, ready for everything to be seen
d put down. He remained tireless-
an enthusiast.*

Margery requested Virginia write his biography, which was published in 1940 by the Hogarth Press. If to her the writing of it felt tedious, many

readers have felt it to be a rather flat recounting of such a vivid person, even 'a masterpiece in self-suppression'. For there is no mention of his lifelong love of her sister, and of their affair, and very little about the suicide of his Breton girlfriend Josette Coatmellec. Interestingly, given Virginia Woolf's own mental condition, she omitted a crucial character trait in Roger, which he fully acknowledges in his own private notes to himself and his musings about Josette. He had a peculiar attraction to an element of strangeness or madness in women. He implies that this was similarly the case in his attraction to his wife Helen Coombe, in whom he found 'a strange touch of genius. And there was beauty too and a certain terror on my part and the mysterious ungetatableness of her – I suppose what became her madness later on, but the terror tho' very definite, so that I felt certain of tragedy when I married, added a fearful delight.' Virginia, in quoting this sentence, omits the key phrase 'certain of tragedy', indicative of her skirting the more problematic topics (*Roger Fry*, pp. 94–5; Spalding, *Roger Fry*, p. 61).

Nevertheless, she mused on the biographer's relation to her subject, writing in her diary about the strange companionship she felt with him through doing this book. 'What a curious relation is mine with Roger at this moment – who have given him a kind of shape after his death – was he like that? I feel very much in his presence at the moment: as if I were intimately connected with him; as if we together had given birth to this vision of him: a child born of us' (*Diary* 5, p. 305). When she sent off her manuscript to Margery, she felt like the merest schoolgirl turning in her paper, and promptly came down with a sore throat and fever. Leonard thought it had no point of view, and was therefore both flawed and dull, with a great many 'dead quotations'. But Margery was, unsurprisingly, delighted: 'It's *him*,' she responded (*Diary* 5, p. 272). And Virginia knew, all along, how contemporary readers would find him important: as she wrote to Margery Fry, the more she read him, the surer she was 'of his lasting' (Banks, *Modern Fiction Studies*, p. 202). Perhaps her struggle in writing the book was worth it. 'I can't help thinking I've caught a good deal of that iridescent man in my oh so laborious butterfly net' (*Diary* 5, p. 266).

*...nessa Bell and Angelica Bell*
*...rnett. Angelica Garnett, a*
*...inter, has inherited her mother's*
*...d father's artistic talent. Angelica*
*...ys of her mother that she would*
*...ve been happy anywhere, on*
*...desert island, with her black*
*...ffee and her paints (conversation,*
*...90). Nevertheless, her palette*
*...rkened considerably after the loss*
*...Julian in the Spanish Civil War.*

# Virginia Woolf and Her Mind

The most unforgettable verbal portrait of Virginia was given by
her niece Angelica Garnett, who perfectly captured in words, in her
*Recollections*, just that face we see represented in so many places
and increasingly iconized. It is a portrait of high mental activity and
physical nervousness:

> *Even at rest ... her attitude was far from sitting, it was striding;*
> *long narrow thighs and shins in long tweed skirts, loping over*
> *the Downs ... or through the London traffic. She was never*
> *placid, never quite at rest ... shadowy temples over which*
> *stretched a transparent skin showing threads of blue; the*

80   Virginia Woolf

*wrinkled waves of her high, narrow forehead; the tautness of those sardonic lips pulled downwards at the corner; her bladed nose, like the breastbone of a bird or the wing of a bat, surmounted by deeply hooded melancholy grey-green eyes. She had the worn beauty of a hare's paw (Marder,* The Measure of Life, *p. 29).*

From early on, her gestures, like her moods, were often in excess, and her neediness of affection would cause her to demand a series of kisses, frequently embarrassing to Vanessa, from whom they were most often demanded.

Virginia's plunges and rises in mood were inescapable. But, always prey to overexcitement, she could never count on her happiness. Leonard would keep close watch, at Monk's House, as elsewhere, and when she became too voluble, would lead her away. As she herself said, she could never 'glory sweepingly' in any mood, for she would tumble from it (*Diary* 4, p. 245). At one moment, she would exclaim, to others and herself, 'Where shall we go? How happy I am,' and, at the next, be submerged in those waters of melancholy never so far away. She often felt 'at sea', as she wrote to T. S. Eliot, swept into the waves. Early on, when her suicidal depressions had declared themselves, after Julia's death and subsequently, Vanessa would exclaim how mad 'the Goat' was, how incapable of taking care of herself, and how Leonard would not be able for long to persist in looking after her: the strain would be too great (Lee, *Virginia Woolf*, p. 181).

In her crises, Virginia Woolf would go through the various and exhausting stages of excitement, hostility and self-accusations. She had been treated, in 1913–15, with the infamous milk diet, supposed to calm one down: she was forced to consume every day four or five pints. Her pathetic notes to Leonard from her bed during these treatments read like a child's plaint: 'I keep thinking of you and

*ndham Lewis, portrait of Virginia olf, 1921. There was not a great l of love lost between the author he Apes of God, who called self 'The Enemy', and the omsberries – yet this pen-and-ink trait captures Woolf's intellectu- y with precision, as she is seated n Edith Sitwell position.*

***Overleaf*** *VW in chair by door in the upstairs room. Photograph by Duncan Grant in the 1930s. 'What's I?' (*Mrs Dalloway, *p. 108).*

want to get to you ... I have been very good ... Its all my fault ... I am grateful and repentant'; 'I really don't think I can stand much more of this ...' (Lee, *Virginia Woolf*, p. 185). Her excruciating sensitivity would render her ill even at the simplest absorption of the mildest drugs. She would become ill for three weeks even after taking only a partial dose of Somnifène, a sea-sickness drug, that Vanessa would give her for the ferry crossing to the Continent. In 1922, she even had a few teeth pulled, for the doctors thought this might lower her temperature.

From her 28 March 1929 diary comes a frank statement of her own dangerous intensity: 'Only in myself, I say, forever bubbles this

**Above** *Virginia Woolf to Ethel Smyth. 'How can I cure my viole moods? I wish you'd tell me. And her own answer: 'Work, work work. That's my final presumptic* (Diary 5, p. 50).

impetuous torrent … I am more full of shape & colour than ever. I think I am bolder as a writer. I am alarmed by my own cruelty with my friends' (*Diary* 3, p. 15). And two and a half years later, in October 1932, aged fifty, she felt 'just poised to shoot forth quite free straight undeflected my bolts whatever they are … I don't believe in aging. I believe in forever altering one's aspect to the sun. Hence my optimism' (*Diary* 4, p. 125). It would be hard to find a writer whose aspects did alter as much as those Virginia Woolf turned to the sun and to her work.

So violent and so apparent were her mood swings that she feared she might be thought not just a difficult writer, but a crazed one. Repeatedly, wherever she was, she would succumb to various crises: at a restaurant, she would faint and have to be led out by Clive, as one day at the Ivy, or whoever was around. She would feel it coming on, and then it would render her incapable of normal behaviour. Virginia's older and adoring composer friend Ethel Smyth, aged seventy-two when Virginia was in her early fifties, would refer to the volcano Virginia was always walking on (Lee, *Virginia Woolf*, p. 595). Virginia was no less clear-eyed about herself. She would question Smyth as she would her other friends on the same topic, wondering how she might control and even cure her moods with their violent manic-depressive alternations. 'O such despairs, and wooden hearted long droughts … and then d'you know walking last evening, in a rage, through Regents Park alone, I became so flooded with exstasy … ' (*Letters* 5, p. 399).

She kept watch upon her own moods, particulary after the publication of a book, such as *The Waves*, when the critics were about to comment. She determined to be free of excessive concern over them, strong in her independence of the moment. 'And at about 2 in the morning I am possessed of a remarkable sense of driving ey[e]less strength … let all praise & blame sink to the bottom or float to the top & let me go my ways indifferent. And care for people. And let fly, in life, on all sides' (*Diary* 4, p. 260).

Highly excitable, she was to be watched carefully, even in her own house, for signs of over-animation: Leonard would often take her away to the upstairs room if they seemed ominous. Her

excitement would occur frequently in relation to that writing without which she could not live and in relation to which her tensions would manifest themselves. John Lehman reported when Virginia was telling him the story of Flush in 1932: 'She soon became so excited and hysterical with laughter, that ... she was red in the face and tears were streaming down her cheeks, before she retired incapable of going on' (Lee, *Virginia Woolf*, p. 110).

In 1939, Woolf met Freud, whose psychological treatises she had mocked, although she had always been privileged – or then cursed – with vivid dreams, and often transcribed them. Yet his works made part of the reading matter she would pick up in order to calm herself after the intensity of too many visitors: 'How difficult to make oneself a centre after all the rings a visitor stirs in one ... How difficult to draw in from all

*Above* Jackets by Vanessa Bell for The Waves (1931) – the interweaving of nature and human perception – and Three Guineas (1938) – the manifesto of the woman always an outsider, foreign to the costumes and customs of male institutions.

*Right* James and Alix (Sargent-Florence) Strachey, the translators of Freud. James had been in love with Rupert Brooke, and Alix, a Newnham girl, had attempted to work at the Hogarth Press, but with little success.

those wide ripples & be at home, central. I tried to centre by reading Freud' (*Diary* 5, p. 299).

She responded intensely to the tales of visitors, eager to have every detail of their story. Tale after tale has come to us of her careful interrogation: go more slowly, say exactly what you saw, what you said, she would repeat. Nigel Nicolson, in his *Virginia Woolf*, recalls her close questioning of him as a child. Angelica Garnett describes a tea party at Charleston in 1936, where Virginia was questioning people. Virginia, says Angelica, was 'in high fettle. She sat by Dorothy Bussy all the time

**Above** *Dorothy Strachey Bussy. Lytton's sister, author of* Olivia, *married to the painter Simon Bu* *and in love with André Gide, wh* *brilliant translator she was.*

**Right** *Virginia Woolf with her nephews Quentin and Julian Bell*

and simply fired questions at her. 'Now Dorothy tell me all your London news, as Clive would say. What did you have for breakfast? What parties have you been to? What was it like at the Clarks the other night? Mary Hutchinson went with you? What did she wear?' (Lee, *Virginia Woolf*, p. 6). It was not as if Virginia liked Mary, Clive Bell's lover, who spent so much time at Charleston, but she enjoyed, sometimes with pangs of guilt, the gossip she could associate with her. 'I didn't like Mary; scented, tinted, lewd lipped & blear eyes; & the consciousness that it's the mean side of me that feasts on such garbage; & resentment with her for making me feed on garbage; & she saying sharp things & then hard, & I unable to say out loud: "Well then, why come & sit on my lawn?"' (*Diary* 2, p. 63). But Virginia adored a good gossip.

Virginia had always been given to identifying with the other. When Vanessa was pregnant, her younger sister wrote her to say that she could perfectly imagine what having a child was like. And continued to compare it to giving birth to a novel, determining to use every possible emotion in her writing. When, during the Spanish Civil War, Julian was killed driving an ambulance, Vanessa, submerged in utter despair, was most comforted by Virginia. Vanessa's suffering now caused her to say she would try to be cheerful when she could, but she knew she would never be happy again. 'An incredible suffering – to watch it – an accident, & someone bleeding. Then I thought the death of a child is childbirth again; sitting there listening' (*Diary* 5, p. 104). At the death of Roger Fry in 1934, Vanessa had thought herself unhappy, but nothing matched this. Virginia was her deepest source of comfort, partly from her ability to identify with her sister, and partly because of her own intensities and emotional highs and lows.

The latter were part of what she called her 'angularity' (*Diary* 5, p. 250), part of her absolute determination to make every single moment count, in life and in writing: 'How to make 1 hour and 35 minutes blaze' (*Diary* 4, p. 5). How to waste no time. This was part of her lifelong determination to 'defeat the shrinkage of age. Always take on new things. Break the rhythm &c' (*Diary* 5, p. 248).

And, indeed, she did always take on new things, until the end.

# Virginia Woolf: Reader and Writer

Among all the things that characterize Virginia Woolf, it is clearly her writing instinct that mattered the most: friends, loves, travels, reading, correspondence, conversation – all these were essential, but the most important of all, unsurprisingly, was her writing (*Diary* 5, p. 65): 'One always harnesses oneself by instinct & can't live without the strain.' Probably the most encouraging words proffered by Virginia Woolf to her diary ever were these: 'Writing again!' It might be a day blazing with light, or then, as on 21 May 1935, 'a cold misting day, with the dog Pinka's feet on my blotting paper' just after this beloved creature had died. Even the loss and the chill were to be noticed, written down, valued, as she had noted her fright and exaltation after Roger Fry's funeral the year before. 'Observe perpetually,' Henry James had said (*Diary*, 8 March 1941).

In Virginia Woolf's definition of herself, intense and blazing, she is definitely centred, as in an image from *The Waves* as it is perceived by the quiet Susan. And yet the six figures are clearly parts of Woolf, the writing lady, whose figure recurs, itself centring the poetic novel: 'The lady sits between the two long windows, writing. I see the lady writing. I see the gardeners sweeping, said Susan ... and the solitary is no longer solitary' (*The Waves*, pp. 17, 141). Writing is, in this novel, as personified by Bernard in his last long monologue, a more lasting and more unifying communication even than that wondrous gossip ongoing between friends. It is to that kind of communication that Virginia Woolf had dedicated her whole being, until the birds broke in, singing in Greek, and, feeling her madness recur, she could no longer think.

In her work account, the routine is established. She writes in the first part of the morning, revising before or after lunch, then after tea sees to her diary or her letters, consecrating her evenings to reading or to visitors, all the while knowing that the only way to

**Below** Example of Virginia's handwriting. Letter to Leonard, in one of
her frequent bouts of illness.

Monday.

Asheham

Dearest Mongoose,

To begin with, I am
to say from nurse, that
I have been very good.
add that I have been very
without you — I dont
being left with the
ole creatures — still, they
very kind — We
been cleaning the
drawing room. Its really
ther fun, & makes
desful difference, Even in

fend off thoughts of destruction and sure gloom, the way not to 'have wasted a thought on death', is that writing instinct: 'One ought to work – never to take one's eyes from one's work ...' (*Diary* 2, p. 142). The excitement was, in general, connected with writing, as exemplified in a letter to Ethel Smyth of 16 October 1930:

> After being ill ... so afraid of my own insanity that I wrote Night and Day ... lying in bed, allowed to write only for one half hour a day ... short stories by way of diversion ... I shall never forget the day I wrote 'The Mark on the Wall' – all in a flash, as if flying, after being kept stone breaking for months ... How I trembled with excitement; and then Leonard came in, and I drank my milk, and concealed my excitement, and wrote I suppose another page of that interminable Night and Day (Letters 4, p. 231).

*ove Duncan Grant's photograph Virginia Woolf in chair leaning to ,t, 11 April 1932: 'And so the inim- le day passes. I face up to it with- : any evasion: this has to be lived y to myself' (Diary 4, p. 206).*

Concealment and revelation mark the two poles of her amorous relation to her own writing. For her plunges would often come after completing a manuscript, wondering if Leonard liked it, if others hated it. This was particularly true of *The Waves*, her most difficult book, after writing which she succumbed to a serious depression, 'trembling under the sense of complete failure' (*Diary* 4, p. 43), predicting it marked the decline of her reputation, thinking Hugh Walpole hated the book, and fearing Leonard's verdict. But Leonard proclaims (*Diary* 4, p. 36): 'It is a masterpiece, and the best of your books', John Lehmann says (*Diary* 4, p. 44): 'I loved it, truly loved it, all the speed of prose & the intensity of poetry', Forster has the 'excitement over it which comes from one's believing that one has encountered a classic' (*Diary* 4, p. 52), and Goldie Dickinson proclaims (*Diary* 4, p. 199): 'Such prose has never been written and it also belongs to here and now though it is dealing also with a theme that is perpetual and universal.' Her own poetic eyeless book this was to be, and that had to stand, even as she was besieged with doubts: she felt disliked, laughed at, but determined to leap over all the fences – like a racehorse – with gallantry. It was, after all, was it not, 'my first book in my own style' (*Diary* 4, p. 53). True, some would consider her mad: it did not really matter. For her, what mattered, as she knew when she was able to shrug off the impulse to listen so vulnerably to outside comments, was that she was trying a shot at her own vision, and that she had to go it alone.

It was to Roger Fry, five months after they had travelled to Greece, that she made a confession which is of primary interest to her readers. She was speaking here, as she often did to Roger, about her reading as it influenced and sometimes impeded her writing. She was, of course, a great reader, and with wide-ranging interests, who spent part of many days reviewing recent books for the press, to bring in a few pounds. She was often an enthusiastic reader of poetry, writing to the poet and novelist Thomas Hardy to laud him for his 'last volume of poems which, to me at any rate, is the most remarkable book to appear in my lifetime' (*Letters* 2, p. 58). She would read poetry before breakfast, especially from the *Oxford Book of Poetry* (*Letters* 2, p. 124).

*ginia looking into her hat, 1930s.*
*25th May 1932: 'What a terrific*
*acity I have for feeling with pos-*
*ty' (Diary 4, p. 102).*

In her letter to Roger Fry, she states clearly her admiration for Marcel Proust, more than any other modernist. He titillated, she said, her own desire to write – surely the supreme compliment from one writer to another. 'Oh, if I could write like that! I cry. And at the moment such is the astonishing vibration and saturation and intensification that he procures – theres something sexual in it – that I feel I *can* write like that, and seize my pen and then I *can't* write like that.' No one, she continued her acknowledgement of what she termed an obsession with Proust and his language, could stimulate the sources of, the nervousness of, language in her (*Letters* 2, p. 525).

> *And again: My great adventure is really Proust. Well — what*
> *remains to be written after that? … I am in a state of amaze-*
> *ment; as if a miracle were being done before my eyes. How,*
> *at last, has someone solidified what has always escaped —*
> *and made it too into this beautiful and perfectly enduring sub-*
> *stance? One has to put the book down and gasp. The pleasure*
> *becomes physical — like sun and wine and grapes and perfect*
> *serenity and intense vitality combined. Far otherwise is it*
> *with Ulysses, to which I bend myself like a martyr to the stake,*
> *and have thank God, now finished — my martyrdom is over'*
> (Letters 2, p. 566).

With some authors she had a difficult time, James Joyce in particular. She noted, in 1918 and 1919, the problems not only of his egotism, but also with his way of writing; if she grew to admire it increasingly, she never felt he was as readable as the authors she truly loved: Jane Austen, John Ruskin, Marcel Proust.

Each reading was, like her travels, the subject of a diary entry, a review, or a letter. Nothing went to waste from what she did, read, or thought. From Henry James she had learned this, as so much else. Be someone on whom nothing is lost, he had said, insisting that the '"moral" sense of a work of art' depended on how much 'felt life' it took to produce it (James, *The Art of the Novel*, pp. 45–6l).

# Virginia and Bloomsbury

Virginia Woolf was a constant friend, and was surrounded by friends, some associated with the Bloomsbury group and some not. We are fortunate in having so much of her correspondence, carried on every day and essential to her way of relating to others. Her relations, epistolary and conversational, had often a palpably sensual warmth and flirtatious intimacy. This sort of correspondence, both oral and written, is one of the main features of the Bloomsbury group, and among its main attractions. About what we think of now as the group itself, Virginia remained sufficiently sanguine. 'If six people, with no special start except what their wits give them, come to dominate, there must be some reason in it … a view of life … rather ascetic and austere indeed; which still holds, and keeps them dining together, and staying together, after 20 years; and no amount of quarrelling or success or failure has altered this' (*Letters* 3, p. 181). The group, however we define it, was clearly her central focus. There were, of course, in it, friends she preferred to others. Virginia was particularly fond of the brilliant Lytton Strachey, with his high-pitched voice and laugh and mordant wit. Among her other five proposals from men associated with Cambridge, there was, on 17 February 1909, Lytton's. He had written to Leonard Woolf, whom she eventually married, not to be surprised if he married Virginia. The idea lasted one day. She was twenty-seven, entranced by his wit, and not in love with him. Nor he, clearly, with her: 'It would be death if she accepted me,' he said (Lee, *Virginia Woolf*, p. 259). So they remained friends always, throughout his multiple relationships, and his eventual settling down with Dora Carrington, the painter who so loved him.

Sometimes, to Virginia's delight, Lytton would appear without his bevy, as she called it, of Ralph Partridge, whom Lytton loved, and others. Then they might, as Virginia wrote to Vita in 1927, stay up very late, she and Lytton, to talk about everything, from love and

sodomy to Queen Elizabeth, the *Antigone*, and *Othello* (*Letters* 5, p. 626). As Virginia wrote in her diary of October 1924, she had been 'right to be in love with him 12 or 15 years ago ... It is an exquisite symphony his nature when all the violins get playing as they did the other night; so deep, so fantastic. We rambled easily.' That was the height of joy for her, to meander among subjects without any preconceived notions.

Above all, she adored being confided in, and so all three – Lytton, Dora Carrington (who was simply called Carrington) and Ralph – all did so. Virginia, excelling in visual portraits, painted them so (*Diary* 2, p. 148): 'Lytton is ripe like a peach in the sun. Carrington wears his old over-

*Above* Carrington's celebrated portrait of Lytton Strachey Reading, late 1916. Learned and witty, Lytton Strachey preferred always to be reading in his portraits. '... have I ever told you before – your appearance. I love it so much' (11 May 1919, Carrington to Strachey). 'I should like to go on always painting you each week ... and never never showing you what I paint' (Carrington, Letters, p. 52).

**ow** *Lytton Strachey at Ham*
*ray House. It was at Ham*
*ray that Carrington lived with*
*ton, after Tidmarsh. 'Everything*
*ok at brings back a memory of*
*... oh darling did you know how*
*dored you. I feared often to tell*
*... I knew you didn't want to feel*
*dependent on you' (Carrington,*
*ers, p. 483).*

Dora Carrington, Ralph
~~ridge~~, Lytton Strachey and
~~ver~~ Strachey at Garsington.
~~on~~ to Virginia: Oh yes, this is
~~~at~~ matters – one's friends' (Diary
~~.~~ 126).

**ht** Carrington, photographed in
~~4~~ by Lytton Strachey. Carrington
~~ed~~ Lytton Strachey, but married
~~ph~~ Partridge because she thought
~~~on~~ did not love her, and to
~~ure~~ that Ralph, whom Lytton
~~nd~~ very attractive, would be near.
~~m~~ not strong enough to live in
~~s~~ world of people and paint'
~~~er~~ Book') Virginia, 18 March
~~2.~~ 'Talk of Carrington: how long
~~ll~~ we talk of Carrington?' (Diary
~~.~~ 85).

coat cut down. Partridge laughs at the wrong jokes.' Carrington, whose woodcuts for the Hogarth Press publication of *Two Stories* she admired greatly, Virginia invited twice to dinner, attracted by her round face, blonde hair and blue eyes, even as she found her somewhat shrivelled up, shabby, and small, wearing her petticoat and jacket that Virginia found 'stupid'. Regrettably, Virginia must have given Ralph, consciously or not, the impression that Lytton cared only little for Carrington, an impression that Ralph repeated the same night to Carrington in bed. She then wrote a heartbreaking letter of farewell to Lytton, and married Ralph, who was rapidly unfaithful to her. Virginia felt 'slightly responsible for that marriage', and also had the feeling 'that one is hauling up a life belt – leaving Carrington to flounder in the middle of the channel embraced by a cuttlefish' (*Letters* 2, p. 595).

Carrington, who was bisexual, and had a particular adoration of the beautiful blue-eyed Henrietta Bingham, the daughter of the American Ambassador to France, and a few other women, continued to carry on an affair with Gerald Brenan, who would write her constant letters. On his part, Ralph fell in love with Frances Marshall, whom he was to marry when Carrington committed suicide, exactly six weeks after Lytton died of stomach cancer in 1932. How could she live without her beloved Lytton? She had already tried to commit suicide by carbon monoxide fumes, hoping her death might be exchanged for his. Virginia commented sadly on Lytton's death. She had admired Lytton's writing immensely, particularly as she read more of 'other peoples lives and essays. He had mastered the art of saying what he meant – and in prose how difficult that is! They remain stated finished controlled – even those little biographies of his. Lord, how I wish he'd lived ... ' as she wrote to her nephew Julian Bell (Banks, *Modern Fiction Studies*, pp. 190–91).

Virginia and Leonard had been the last people to see Carrington, who had run into Virginia's arms, and had read Virginia's moving letter to her just before putting on Lytton's dressing gown and pulling the trigger. 'Oh but Carrington we have to live and be ourselves – and I feel it is more for you to live than for any one; because he loved you so, and loved your oddities and the way you have of being yourself' (*Letters* 5, p. 31). Carrington was to reply on 4 February, 'There are only a few letters that have been of any use. Yours most of all, because you understand' (Caws, *Women of Bloomsbury*, p. 61). Virginia understood a great deal, and Carrington's suicide haunted her for a long time.

Virginia was particularly gifted with the power to admire others. She especially admired Maynard Keynes – who had been Duncan's companion in Fitzroy Square, and always had his room

en Raverat, John Maynard
nes. 'I have to admit that,
liant as Lytton was, Maynard
s the more brilliant' – Steven
nciman (Holroyd, Lytton
achey, p. 1018).

at Charleston. Perhaps she admired him more than she liked him, finding him sceptical and inhuman, 'sensual, brutal, unimaginative, very thick and Opulent'. With his clearly 'remarkable mind', his conversation was mainly about politics and about the 'great financial crisis', neither of great interest for her. She also considered him condescending to his wife, the former ballerina with the Ballets Russes, Lydia Lopokova, who was equally irritating to Vanessa and Virginia, interrupting their work in her thickly accented English with conversation they found childish in the extreme.

**Left** *Lydia Lopokova practising, probably at 46 Gordon Square, London, 1925. Lydia, who had bee[n] a principal ballerina, with the Ballets Russes, was the wife of Joh[n] Maynard Keynes.*

Another of her admirations, a great friend from the moment they met, was the novelist E. M. Forster, whom she thought of as pale blue. In 1919, he struck her as 'an unworldly, transparent character, whimsical & detached, caring very little I should think what people say … he resembles a vaguely rambling butterfly, since there is no intensity or rapidity about him' (*Diary* 1, p. 295). They would spend many hours discussing their reading and writing. It was through Forster's Provençal translator and the close friend of Roger Fry, Charles Mauron, that the Frenchman came over to England in 1936 and 1937, where he stayed with Forster and visited Charleston with his first wife, Marie.

At first, Virginia found Mauron heavy and relatively uninteresting: 'that blind Frenchman,' she called him. Later, when she had so delighted in his psychoanalytic comments (more properly, psycho-critical, to give credit to the school he founded) on the poems of

*ve Charles Mauron and his
d friend E. M. Forster at the
uron home on the Avenue Van
h, photo by Alice Mauron.
rles Mauron was translating
vards End and Room with a
v. He also translated Orlando
the central part of To The
thouse, as well as texts of
ry James and T. E. Lawrence.*

Mallarmé that Roger had translated with Julian
Bell, she wrote to him, after Roger's death. He
was, she alleged, the critic who best understood
what Roger had meant to the world of aesthetics
and to them all. Mauron, with his wife Marie, had
been close to Julian Bell, who had spent a good
deal of time with them at the small house, the
Mas d'Angirany, that they had shared with Roger
Fry. It was Mauron who had written the most convincing letters to plead with Julian not to go off
to the war in Spain, where he was killed. And so he was always a
close friend to the Bloomsbury group, their 'man in France', as
they called him.

**Above** *Photograph of Charles
and Marie Mauron at Charleston.
The Maurons shared their house in
St Remy, the Mas d'Angirany, with
Roger Fry.*

**Right** *Lytton Strachey and Virginia
Woolf at Garsington, 1923. Ottoline
Morrell and her husband Philip gath-
ered around them at Garsington
the members of the Bloomsbury
circle and other writers and artists:
'Brainy talk.' The gatherings were
full of French chatter, inspired by
the Francophile Roger Fry, who had
a brief fling with Ottoline Morrell.*

Virginia kept in touch with others who were only loosely associated with the Bloomsbury circle, such as the socialite Ottoline Morrell, who had parties devoted more to group conversation than Virginia's quieter times, with smaller numbers, at her far smaller Monk's House. During the war, the large home of Ottoline and Philip Morrell, Garsington, had been a perfect place to house a group of conscientious objectors. This sometimes quarrelsome group included Clive, Lytton, Aldous Huxley, Virginia's friend and the only writer she felt a rivalry with, Katherine Mansfield and her often unfaithful partner Middleton Murry, as well as the painters Dorothy Brett and Mark Gertler, and the writers Siegfried Sassoon and D.H. Lawrence.

*Above*  Simon Bussy, Vanessa Bel and Duncan Grant at Garsington Ottoline and Philip Morrell had to sell the estate in 1928.

At Garsington with the Morrells, games were played, elaborate costumes were worn, and the hostess dressed in sumptuous and startling gowns. Ottoline's husband, Philip, made several unwelcome approaches to Virginia over the years, in 1917, 1927, and

*bove* Simon Bussy's 1920 painting
*Lady* Ottoline Morell, the colour-
*and* brilliantly dressed Ottoline,
*chantress of Bloomsbury'* as
*ginia Woolf called her (Letters 3,*
*565). 'A brave spirit, unbroken/*
*ighting in beauty and goodness/*
*d the love of her friends' (Virginia*
*olf and T. S. Eliot – original lines*
*her tomb). The philosopher*
*trand Russell was in love with her*
*years.*

1928, just before his death. The lives of Virginia and Ottoline were interconnected over many years and, although they were immensely different, they shared many friends. Ottoline had, famously, been loved for years by the philosopher Bertrand Russell, and had had a brief involvement with Roger Fry, about which he spoke freely, and she, less so, blaming him for a great deal of malicious gossip. To Virginia, Ottoline, so improbably tall, seemed a kind of fancy-dress character, with her outlandish hats and her nasal drawl, 'with a huge head of copper-coloured hair, turquoise eyes and great beaky features … fantastical high-coloured clothes and hats …' (Lee, *Virginia Woolf*, p. 175). Everything about the décor of Garsington at that period seems stagey in the extreme, both colours and textures. The brocades were all pink and pale yellows. Ottoline seemed always to be 'what I most am: very rapid, excited, amused, intense' (*Diary*, 4, p. 260), said Virginia, 'bearing down on one from afar in her white shawl with the great scarlet flowers on it and sweeping one away from the large room and the crowd into a little room with her alone, where she plied one with questions that were so intimate and so intense ….' (*Moments*, p. 217).

Writing gossipy letters to family and friends was one of Virginia's finest and funniest pastimes. So, writing to Duncan about Ottoline (*Letters* 2, p. 422), she describes her most unkindly, saying in what 'fine feather' she was speaking of one of Duncan's exhibitions: 'The poor old thing undulated and eulogized till really it was like talking to some poor fowl in delirium – her neck became long and longer and you know how she always hangs to "wonderful" as if it were a rope dangling in her vacuum –' In later years, when Ottoline grew deaf, and used (like Molly McCarthy, another member of the Bloomsbury group, and like her painter friend Dorothy Brett) a very large ear trumpet, she would compare her, both stoical and shy, to a Renaissance princess. In any case, the conversation at Garsington was always easy and aesthetic, a topic for Virginia's gentle parody: she would picture Clive and Ottoline, sitting at tea, talking and talking, and proclaiming the end of Western civilization (*Letters* 2, p. 51).

⁊ *Virginia Woolf at Garsington.*

**Left and right** Late photographs of Virginia Woolf by Gisèle Freund, 1939. 'What one envies more than anything is simply life' (Diary 2, p. 158).

## Closer: Virginia's Expressing Herself

Virginia's masterpiece, *The Waves*, as she spoke of it to Goldesworthy Lowes Dickinson, who wrote to say what a beautiful poem it was, offers an interior portrait of the author as convincing as that in any biography, short or long. To him, she wrote: 'The six characters were supposed to be one. I'm getting old myself – I shall be fifty next year; and I come to feel more and more how difficult it is to collect oneself into one Virginia' (*Letters* 4, p. 397). It was,

*Late photograph of Virginia Woolf by Man Ray. 15 May 1940: 'Think is my fighting' (Diary 5, p. 285).*

always, a matter of holding on to her sense of continuity, with others and with herself. As she had remarked on the problems of friendship and singleness of spirit, all of it had to be contained, or constructed, into one whole.

And to Vita, Virginia remained close in her mind and her letters. Their correspondence enlightens us about Virginia's relation not just to her close friends, to her sexual sensuality, but to writing. For far from being able to enunciate aloud her own sentiments, Virginia Woolf found herself constantly in astonishing difficulty over them, for someone whose writing is so acutely able to express, seemingly, all sentiments, emotions and sensualities. She, who cared so intensely about language, phrasing, and the exact correspondence between what we say and mean and feel, constantly longed for some more subtle fashion of marking the distinction between the nuances of her words and meanings. As she wrote and reiterated to Vita: 'I must buy some shaded inks lavenders, pinks, violets – to shade my meaning I see I gave you many wrong meanings, using only black ink … No no, I must buy my coloured inks … But no, I must get my coloured inks' (*Letters* 6, pp. 461–2). This was crucial in friendships of all kinds, in particular in those we could think of as bearing the colour of love. It seems absolutely fitting that the key passage on coloured inks should have been addressed to Vita.

From the time Virginia wrote to Vita (*Letters* 4, p. 13): 'You are still the only face I have in my minds eye', through the time, in 1940, when bombs were exploding around her house, and Virginia thought that 'she might be killed any moment', she was forthrightly affectionate with this great friend. 'What can one say – except that I love you and I've got to live through this strange quiet evening thinking of you sitting there alone … You have given me such happiness' and, as a postscript, 'Ring me up any time' (*Letters* 6, p. 424). And, writing to Vita (*Letters* 6, p. 476), she says, feelingly: 'I suppose your orchard is beginning to dapple as it did the day I came there. One of the sights I shall see on my death bed.'

Leonard was the emotional anchor for such continuity as any living person could provide. Being alone with Leonard she continued to

*Photo by Virginia Woolf on the same day in 1932 of Leonard Woolf and Vita Sackville-West with dogs. Vita to Virginia, 30 March 1928: 'A very good life, Virginia.' So it was.*

discover new depths of 'warmth, curiosity, attachment' (*Diary* 6, p. 320). That was after nineteen years of marriage. And six years later, she found that, after twenty-five years, they still could not bear separation. Each day, after dinner, as they would settle down to their reading: 'Are you in your stall, brother? – well, what can trouble this happiness? And every day is necessarily full of it' (*Diary* 6, p. 320). Their marriage, like their friendships, was full of 'brainy talk'; their companionship, full of companionable perceptions. It was, as nearly as we can imagine, a perfect setting for work and for love.

To look through Virginia's diary is to see, page after page, year after year, both the exaltation of extreme alertness and the struggle to note it all, while swimming in her 'dark green depths' (*Diary* 3, p. 255). Often, the very perception is enhanced by the desperate desire to notice and to note:

> *The sun streams (no: never streams floods rather ) down upon*
> *all the yellow fields & the long low barns; & what wouldn't I*
> *give to be coming through Firle woods, dusty & hot, with my*
> *nose turned home, every muscle tired, & the brain laid up in*
> *sweet lavender, so sane & cool, & ripe for the morrow's task.*
> *How I should notice everything – the phrase for it coming the*
> *moment after & fitting like a glove; & then on the dusty road,*
> *as I ground my pedals, so my story would begin telling itself;*
> *& then the sun would be down, & home, & some bout of poetry*
> *after dinner, half read, half lived, as if the flesh were dissolved*
> *& through it the flowers burst red & white* (Diary *2, p. 133).*

This was the sun of August, at its height. Over the years, in the frequent gloom of England – that gloom she had dreamed of escaping every year, during the brief reverie of having her own house in the Midi of France – it was, like this, often the infrequent sun streaming down that would most excite her, in whatever month. So a September sun would leave her feeling exalted: 'I will canter here a moment' (*Diary* 3, p. 256), and a May sun no less so: 'On whit Monday the sun blazed, making the grass semitransparent. And space leisure seemed to lie all about; & I said, not once in an extasy, but frequently & soberly, This is happiness' (*Diary* 4, p. 27).

But it did not require the sun. Simply being with Leonard was enough. They were so content, she reiterated in her diaries and letters, experiencing every day some form of high contentment, just with their ordinary life: cooking dinner and playing bowls on the lawn and reading (*Diary* 5, p. 231). 'But oh, the happiness of this life … I was thinking to myself today, few people in Cheapside can be

saying "It is too good to be true – that L. & I are going to dine alone tonight'" (*Diary* 5 p. 53).

One of her own reflections early on, after her marriage of, then, thirteen years, holds, I think, the clue to some deep inwardness, in herself and between herself and Leonard, neither to be explained, nor explained away. It implies the true centre of the continuity she so needed between the parts of her being.

> *I have a child's trust in Leonard ... the core of my life, which is this complete comfort with Leonard ... the immense success of our life is I think, that our treasure is hid away; or rather in such common things that nothing can touch it* (Diary 4, pp. 29–30).

ads of Virginia and Leonard
olf, in Monk's House garden.

The endurance of the writing, and of that writing life, is kept still in those common things and things perceived in common: sunlight and fog, working times, she in her studio and he at his desk, and then times of playing bowls in the garden where now the two heads of Leonard and Virginia keep watch – Virginia's eyes are open, Leonard's closed. On the base of Virginia's there is inscribed the last line of *The Waves* about Perceval, Thoby, and indeed Virginia: 'Against you I will fling myself, unvanquished and unyielding, O Death!' (*The Waves*, p. 297).

# Leaving: the Ouse

In May 1940, England had been, for a while now, under the menace
of war. As a Jew, Leonard was in imminent danger should there be
an invasion, as in France, and Virginia felt they should be prepared.
They had poison ready. On 15 May, Virginia wrote in her diary the
fearful words: 'If England defeated: What point in waiting? Better
shut the garage doors' (*Diary* 5, p. 284). The atmosphere weighed
heavily on both of them, and particularly on her.

She had been haunted for years, like Rhoda in *The Waves*, by that
deep water imagery that came to her mind in moments of severe
depression, such as that of 10 June 1929, when she wrote about
that novel and the feeling of drowning:

> *Lord, how deep it is … Directly I stop working I feel that I am
> sinking down, down. And as usual, I feel that if I sink further
> I shall reach the truth. That is the only mitigation; a kind of
> nobility. Solemnity. I shall make myself face the fact that there
> is nothing – nothing for any of us. Work, reading, writing are
> all disguises; & relations with people. Yes, even having children
> would be useless (Diary 3, p. 235).*

Over and over, the wave would rise, always about to engulf her:

> *Oh its beginning its coming – the horror – physically like a
> painful wave swelling about the heart – tossing me up. I'm
> unhappy unhappy! Down – God, I wish I were dead. Pause.
> But why am I feeling this? Let me watch the wave rise. I
> watch. Vanessa. Children. Failure, yes; I detect that. Failure
> failure. (The wave rises.) Oh they laughed at my taste in green
> paint! Wave crashes. I wish I were dead! I've only a few years
> to live I hope. I can't face this horror any more – (this is the
> wave spreading out over me).*

In 1940, the Ouse river burst through its banks, unleashing a flood

**ve** Virginia Woolf's writing
*io* in the garden. 'And so I go on
*ippose that the shock-receiving
icity is what makes me a writer*
*make it real by putting it*
*words. It is only by putting*
*to words that I make it whole;*
*wholeness means that it has*

*lost its power to hurt me; it gives*
*me, perhaps because by doing so I*
*take away the pain, a great delight*
*to put the severed parts together.*
*Perhaps this is the strongest pleasure*
*known to me . . . making a scene*
*come right; making a character*
*come together'* (Moments, p. 72).

of white water that covered the fields over which Virginia looked from her writing table in the garden studio, all the way to her back gate. She described the sight: of the yellowed land, the red roofs, and the trees deprived of leaves. This desolate and savage state of nature seemed to be straight out of the middle ages, as she put it (*Letters* 6, p. 424), and yet not very distant from her and her writing. The state continued.

Because of her visibly intense depression, the psychiatrist Octavia Wilberforce was called in. As Wilberforce later described it in a letter to her friend Elizabeth Robins (Marder, *The Measure of Life*, p. 337), it was a difficult situation, since Virginia kept saying repeatedly how unnecessary it was for her to have come. Wondering what she should or could have done, the doctor described what a rocky business it had been discussing anything at that point. She quotes herself in her own understandable awkwardness, faced with the despairing Virginia:

> O: *'You have no idea how much I enjoy coming over, how it helps talking to an – er – outsize mind … Oh I cant say what I want' … 'Oh but do try – I want to know. You don't know how much I need it' and eyes me gravely and steadily.*

Octavia realized too late that she might perhaps have helped Virginia, had she been able to involve her in something other than her mental solitude. Virginia had asked if she could not help Octavia in some way, perhaps cataloguing her books? But, continued Octavia, had it all transpired in that other fashion and then ended like this as it was perhaps bound to, 'Wouldn't it have been even worse?' (Marder, *The Measure of Life*, p. 362).

In any case, it was the end now. Certain she was going mad, hearing inside her head a chorus of birds singing in Greek, Virginia had set out a week before to drown herself. But she had been unsuccessful, returning drenched. And now she set out again across the garden, to the river Ouse, weighting down her pockets with stones. Three suicide notes were found by Leonard, one saying to Vanessa how much she and the children

nk's House, the elms (named nard and Virginia) in the snow. en 'Virginia' was struck by light- g, the other also fell.

had meant: 'I think you know', wrote Virginia (*Letters* 6, p. 485).

*Above* Virginia Woolf with hat or grass and statue.

For Leonard, a letter left on the writing pad in her studio begins: 'I want to tell you that you have given me complete happiness', and another, found in their sitting room, ends, 'Everything has gone from me but the certainty of your goodness. I can't go on spoiling your life any longer. I don't think two people could have been happier than we have been' (*Letters* 6, pp. 486, 481). The words remain after her, leaving from beginning to end an inescapable memory of mutual and mutually recognized love.

*Leonard Woolf with pipe and statue.*
*'But oh, the happiness of this life ...*
*I was thinking to myself today, few*
*people in Cheapside can be saying*
*"It is too good to be true – that*
*Leonard & I are going to dine alone*
*tonight"' (Diary 5, p. 53).*

I want to finish accordingly not with a tragic view of the conclusion of Virginia's life, but with her own intense perception of it and of herself. A note she wrote not to Leonard or Vanessa but to herself, on 8 March 1941, sums up best both her life and her writing, as I see them. It links her with that other great observer whom she so respected, and whose wisdom she knew, in her writing and her life, how to use:

> No I intend no introspection. I mark Henry James' sentence: Observe perpetually. Observe the oncome of age. Observe greed. Observe my own despondency. By that means it becomes serviceable. Or so I hope. I insist upon spending this time to the best advantage. I will go down with my colours flying.

And so she did.

# Chronology

1882    Born Adeline Virginia Stephen, in London at Hyde Park Gate, daughter of Leslie Stephen and Julia Prinsep Duckworth; childhood in London and St Ives.

1895    Julia Duckworth dies. The first of Virginia's early breakdowns and recoveries.

1896    Virginia Stephen and her elder sister Vanessa travel to northern France with their half-brother George Duckworth and his aunt Minnie Duckworth.

1904    Leslie Stephen dies. Virginia has a second breakdown, then she, Vanessa and their brother Adrian settle into 46 Gordon Square.

1905    Duncan Grant meets Vanessa Stephen through Pippa, one of Lytton Strachey's sisters.

1906    Virginia, Vanessa, Adrian and their brother Thoby travel to Greece. Thoby contracts typhoid and dies; Vanessa accepts a marriage proposal from Clive Bell. Before Vanessa's marriage, Virginia and Adrian move to Fitzroy Square; Roger Fry takes up his curatorship of the Department of Paintings at the Metropolitan Museum in New York.

1907    Virginia goes with Clive, Leonard, Vanessa and Adrian to Paris; Clive and Vanessa marry.

1909    Virginia receives proposal of marriage from Lytton Strachey, considers it for one evening.

1910    Virginia, Adrian and Duncan Grant take part in the Dreadnought Hoax; Roger Fry's appointment at the Metropolitan is terminated because of a disagreement with J. Pierpont Morgan: he meets Clive and Vanessa Bell on the railway platform at Cambridge, about to take the London train; he arranges the 'Manet and the Post-Impressionist Exhibition' at the Grafton Gallery in London; gradual gathering of the Bloomsbury group.

1911     Vanessa goes to Turkey with Clive Bell, Roger Fry and Harry Norton; Vanessa and Roger begin their affair.

1912     Virginia marries Leonard Woolf in August; they find Asheham.

1913     Virginia has a third mental breakdown and attempts suicide.

1914     First World War begins.

1915     Publication of *The Voyage Out*; Virginia has another breakdown.

1916     John Maynard Keynes moves to 46 Gordon Square, in which Vanessa Bell and Duncan Grant have rooms; (Dora) Carrington falls in love with Lytton Strachey; Vanessa discovers Charleston Farmhouse.

1917     Virginia and Leonard rent Hogarth House in Richmond and set up the Hogarth Press.

1918     First World War ends; Diaghilev's Ballets Russes arrives in London; Vita Sackville-West and Violet Keppel Trefusis elope to France, and their husbands fly over to bring them back.

1919     Keynes attends Peace Conference; Roger Fry meets Charles and Marie Mauron at Les Baux in Provence; publication of *Night and Day* with Gerald Duckworth, and a collection of short stories with the Hogarth Press.

1921     Carrington marries Ralph Partridge, despairing of Lytton's affection for her; Vanessa and Duncan rent a house in St Tropez; Virginia publishes some short fiction, *Monday or Tuesday*, with the Hogarth Press.

1922     Roger Fry meets Josette Coatmellec at the Coué Clinic; Virginia meets Vita Sackville-West at a dinner; publication of *Jacob's Room*; Virginia and Leonard go to Spain to visit Gerald Brenan.

1924     Virginia and Leonard move to Tavistock Square, bringing the Hogarth Press with them; Lytton Strachey buys Ham Spray House, which Carrington will decorate; Ralph is in love with Frances Marshall, whom he will marry after Carrington's suicide; Josette Coatmellec commits suicide, believing Roger to be mocking her.

| 1925 | Virginia and Vita have a brief sexual relationship; Virginia starts *To the Lighthouse*; publication of *The Common Reader*; publication of *Mrs Dalloway*; Virginia and Leonard visit Cassis; Ralph and Frances set up house together; Jacques Raverat dies. |
|------|------|
| 1927 | Publication of *To the Lighthouse*; Virginia starts *Orlando*; Virginia and Leonard return to Cassis, stay at Hotel Cendrillon; Duncan and Vanessa acquire lease of La Bergère, near Fontcreuse just outside of Cassis. |
| 1928 | Virginia and Leonard arrive in their Singer car to visit Vanessa and Duncan in Cassis; later on they return to Cassis by train, and consider buying La Boudarde. |
| 1929 | Publication of *A Room of One's Own*. |
| 1931 | Publication of *The Waves*. |
| 1932 | Lytton Strachey dies; Carrington commits suicide; Virginia, Roger Fry and his sister Margery travel to Greece; publication of *The Common Reader*. |
| 1933 | Virginia and Leonard drive through France, visit the Bussys at Roquebrune; Roger Fry accepts the Slade Professorship at Cambridge; publication of *Flush*. |
| 1934 | Dorothy Bussy shows her novel *Olivia* to André Gide, who dismisses it. Later it is published to great acclaim and Gide repents. |
| 1935 | Virginia's nephew Julian Bell teaches in Wuhan University in China. |
| 1937 | Julian Bell is killed in Spain; Ottoline Morrell dies; Vanessa and Angelica Bell go to Cassis, stay at Fontcreuse because La Bergère is rented; publication of *The Years*. |
| 1938 | Publication of *Three Guineas*. |
| 1939 | Virginia and Leonard go to Brittany and Normandy; war declared on 3 September. |
| 1940 | The Bussys rent La Souco to André Malraux, and stay in Nice, where Matisse has tea with them every afternoon; publication of *Roger Fry*; Virginia's London home destroyed by bombs. |
| 1941 | Virginia walks into the Ouse at Rodmell, with stones in her pocket; publication of *Between the Acts*. |

# Bibliography

*Any references in the text to Virginia Woolf's works are by short title;*
*references to other authors are by author's name and short title.*

Joanne Trautmann Banks, ed., 'Some New Virginia Woolf Letters', *Modern Fiction Studies*, Summer 1984, vol. 30, no. 2.

Quentin Bell, *Elders and Betters (Bloomsbury Recalled)*, (New York: Columbia University Press, 1995).

Vanessa Bell, *Sketches in Pen and Ink: A Bloomsbury Notebook*, ed. Lia Giachero (London: Hogarth Press, 1997).

Carrington, Dora, *Letters and Excerpts from Her Diaries*, ed. David Garnett (London: Jonathan Cape, 1970).

— 'Her Book' [D. C. Patride, sic.], unpublished document (British Library).

— DC/GB Letters of Carrington and Gerald Brenan (Harry Ransom Humanities Research Center).

Mary Ann Caws, *Women of Bloomsbury: Virginia, Vanessa, Carrington* (New York and London: Routledge, 1989).

— , ed., *Vita Sackville-West: Selected Writings*, including the complete *Seducers in Ecuador* and unpublished material from Sissinghurst Castle and the Lilly Library, Bloomington, Indiana. Preface by Nigel Nicolson (London and New York: Palgrave, 2002).

— and Sarah Bird Wright, *Bloomsbury and France: Art and Friends* (New York and Oxford: Oxford University Press, 1999).

— and Nicola Luckhurst, eds, *The Reception of Virginia Woolf in Europe* (London: Continuum Press, 2001).

Angelica Garnett, *Deceived with Kindness: A Bloomsbury Childhood* (Oxford: Oxford University Press, 1984).

— *The Eternal Moment* (Orono, Maine: Puckerbrush Press, 1998).

— *Recollections of Virginia Woolf*, ed. Joan Russell Noble (London: Penguin, 1975).

Gretchen Gerzina, *Carrington: A Life of Dora Carrington* (London: John Murray, 1989; New York: Norton, 1989).

Diane Filby Gillespie, *The Sisters' Arts: The Writing and Painting of Virginia Woolf and Vanessa Bell* (Syracuse: Syracuse University Press, 1988).

Victoria Glendinning, *Vita* (London: Penguin, 1984).

Lyndall Gordon, *A Writer's Life: Virginia Woolf* (New York: Norton, 1984).

Carolyn Heilbrun, *Writing a Woman's Life* (New York: Ballantine Books, 1988).

Michael Holroyd, *Lytton Strachey: The New Biography* (London: Chatto & Windus, 1994; New York: Farrar Straus Giroux, 1995).

Henry James, *The Art of the Novel* (New York: Charles Scribner's, 1934; Boston: Northeastern University Press, 1984).

Hermione Lee, *Virginia Woolf* (London: Chatto & Windus, 1996; New York: Alfred Knopf, 1998).

Jane Marcus, ed., *Virginia Woolf and Bloomsbury* (New York and London: Macmillan, 1987).

Herbert Marder, *The Measure of Life: Virginia Woolf's Last Years* (Ithaca and London: Cornell University Press, 2000).

Regina Marler, *Bloomsbury Pie: The Making of the Bloomsbury Boom* (New York: Henry Holt, 1997).

Nigel Nicolson, *Virginia Woolf* (London and New York: Penguin, 2000).

Marcel Proust, *In Search of Lost Time (Remembrance of Things Past)* (New York: Random House, 1981; Vintage, 1982).

Gwen Raverat Exhibition: New Hall, University of Cambridge, 13 June – 12 July 1998. Fitzwilliam Museum. Catalogue by Gillie Coutts.

Phyllis Rose, *Woman of Letters: A Life of Virginia Woolf* (London: Routledge & Kegan Paul, 1978).

Miranda Seymour, *Ottoline Morrell: Life on the Grand Scale* (New York: Farrar Straus Giroux, 1992).

Frances Spalding, *Roger Fry* (London: Granada, 1980).

— *Vanessa Bell* (London: Macmillan, 1985).

— *Gwen Raverat: Friends, Family and Affections* (London and New York: Harvill, 2001).

Denys Sutton, ed., *Letters of Roger Fry*, 2 vols. (London: Chatto & Windus, 1992).

Leonard Woolf, *Sowing* (London: Hogarth Press, 1960).

— *Growing* (London: Hogarth Press, 1961).

— *Beginning Again* (London: Hogarth Press, 1964).

— *Downhill All the Way* (London: Hogarth Press, 1967).

— *The Journey not the Arrival Matters* (London: Hogarth Press, 1969).

Virginia Woolf, *Flush: A Biography* (New York and London: Harcourt Brace Jovanovich, 1931).

— *Moments of Being: Unpublished Autobiographical Writings*, ed. Jeanne Schulkind (New York: Harcourt, 1985).

— *Orlando: A Biography* (London: Hogarth Press, 1928; Penguin, 1993).

— *Roger Fry: A Biography* (London: Hogarth Press, 1940, 1991).

— *The Waves* (London: Hogarth Press, 1931; New York: Harcourt Brace Jovanovich, 1959; London: Penguin, 1992).

— *The Diary of Virginia Woolf*, ed. Anne Olivier Bell and Andrew McNeillie, 5 vols. (London: Hogarth Press, 1977–84).

— *The Letters of Virginia Woolf*, ed. Nigel Nicolson and Joanne Trautmann Banks, 6 vols. (London: Hogarth Press, 1975–80).

Sarah Bird Wright, *Living at Monk's House* (London: Cecil Woolf Books, 1995).

Alex Zwerdling, *Virginia Woolf and the Real World* (Berkeley: University of California Press, 1986).

# Illustrations

*List of illustrations (by page number) and photographic acknowledge-
ments. Every effort has been made to contact all copyright holders.
The publishers will be happy to make good in future editions any errors
or omissions brought to their attention.*

**1**. Formal family gathering. (The Harvard Theatre Collection, The Houghton
Library, Harvard University, Cambridge, Massachusetts)

**4**. Virginia Woolf, 1902, photo by George Charles Beresford. (By courtesy of the
National Portrait Gallery, London)

**5**. Virginia Woolf, 1912, portrait by Vanessa Bell. (By courtesy of the National
Portrait Gallery, London)

**6**. The Stephens with Virginia. (The Harvard Theatre Collection, The Houghton
Library, Harvard University, Cambridge, Massachusetts)

**9**. Virginia and Vanessa Stephen. (The Harvard Theatre Collection, The
Houghton Library, Harvard University, Cambridge, Massachusetts)

**11** (*left*). Dust jacket for *To the Lighthouse*, designed by Vanessa Bell. (The
Bloomsbury Workshop © 1961 The Estate of Vanessa Bell, courtesy Henrietta
Garnett)

**11** (*right*). Dustjacket for *Mrs Dalloway*, designed by Vanessa Bell. (The
Bloomsbury Workshop © 1961 The Estate of Vanessa Bell, courtesy Henrietta
Garnett)

**12**. *46 Gordon Square*, 1909, painting by Vanessa Bell. (© Estate of Vanessa Bell,
courtesy The Charleston Trust, Lewes)

**14**. Early photograph of Virginia Stephen. (The Harvard Theatre Collection,
The Houghton Library, Harvard University, Cambridge, Massachusetts)

**16–17**. Leonard Woolf, Roger Fry and Virginia Woolf, 1912. (The Harvard Theatre
Collection, The Houghton Library, Harvard University, Cambridge,
Massachusetts)

**19**. Leonard Woolf and Virginia Stephen, *c*.1912. (© Tate Archive)

**20**. Flush. (The Harvard Theatre Collection, The Houghton Library, Harvard
University, Cambridge, Massachusetts)

**22–3**. Janet Case, Virginia Stephen and Vanessa Bell at Firle Park, 1911. (The
Harvard Theatre Collection, The Houghton Library, Harvard University,
Cambridge, Massachusetts)

**24**. Virginia Woolf, portrait by Duncan Grant. (Bridgeman Art Library/Private
Collection/The Bloomsbury Workshop © 1978 The Estate of Duncan Grant,
courtesy Henrietta Garnett)

**26**. Sketch of Virginia Woolf at the Hogarth Press by Richard Kennedy. (Bridgeman Art Library/Private Collection)

**28** (*above*). Asheham. House, 1914, with Leonard Woolf leaning against the wall. (The Harvard Theatre Collection, The Houghton Library, Harvard University, Cambridge, Massachusetts)

**28** (*below*). Lytton Strachey, Duncan Grant and Clive Bell at Asheham, 1913. (© Tate Archive)

**29**. *The Tub*, 1917, painting by Vanessa Bell. (© Tate Gallery and © 1961 The Estate of Vanessa Bell, courtesy Henrietta Garnett)

**30**. Quentin and Julian Bell as young children. (The Harvard Theatre Collection, The Houghton Library, Harvard University, Cambridge, Massachusetts)

**31** (*above*). Vanessa Bell painting at Charleston, c.1936. (© Tate Archive)

**31** (*below*). Duncan Grant, Angelica Bell and Roger Fry at Charleston, 1926. (© Tate Archive)

**32**. John Maynard Keynes and Duncan Grant. (The Harvard Theatre Collection, The Houghton Library, Harvard University, Cambridge, Massachusetts)

**33**. *Still Life with Apples*, painting by Paul Cézanne. (By kind permission of the Provost and Fellows of King's College, Cambridge)

**34**. Gate of Monk's House with dog. (The Harvard Theatre Collection, The Houghton Library, Harvard University, Cambridge, Massachusetts)

**35**. Vanessa Bell's paintings of the lighthouse at Godrevy on fireplace tiles at Monk's House. (Courtesy Sarah Bird Wright)

**36**. Leonard Woolf's study at Monk's House. (Courtesy Sarah Bird Wright)

**37**. Virginia Woolf at Monk's House with John Lehmann. (The Harvard Theatre Collection, The Houghton Library, Harvard University, Cambridge, Massachusetts)

**38**. Virginia Woolf, Charles Mauron and Helen Anrep playing bowls. (The Harvard Theatre Collection, The Houghton Library, Harvard University, Cambridge, Massachusetts)

**40**. T. S. Eliot, Virginia Woolf and Vivien Eliot, 1932. (The Harvard Theatre Collection, The Houghton Library, Harvard University, Cambridge, Massachusetts)

**41**. Ethel Sands at the Château d'Auppegard. (From Wendy Baron, *Miss Ethel Sands and Her Circle* (London: Peter Owen Ltd., 1977))

**42**. Simon Bussy. (Manuscripts Department, Lilly Library, University of Indiana, Bloomington, Indiana)

**43**. André Gide and Dorothy Strachey Bussy, 1922. (From Klara Fassbinder. 'Gide at Pontigny', *Entretiens sur André Gide*, 6–14 September 1964, courtesy Association des Amis de Cerisy)

**44**. Lytton Strachey, 1904, portrait by Simon Bussy. (By courtesy of the National Portrait Gallery, London. Copyright Reserved)

**46**. Dorothy and Janie Bussy. (The Harvard Theatre Collection, The Houghton Library, Harvard University, Cambridge, Massachusetts)

**47**. *Dorothy Bussy at La Souco*, 1954, painting by Vanessa Bell. (© Estate of Vanessa Bell, courtesy The Charleston Trust, Lewes)

**48**. *Vanessa Bell Painting at La Souco*, 1960, by Duncan Grant. (© Estate of Duncan Grant, courtesy The Charleston Trust, Lewes)

**49** (*left*). Jacques Raverat. (The Harvard Theatre Collection, The Houghton Library, Harvard University, Cambridge, Massachusetts)

**49** (*right*). Gwen Darwin Raverat, photo by Sophie Gurney. (From *Virginia Woolf: Lettres Illustrés*)

**50**. Duncan Grant and Vanessa Bell at La Bergère, photograph by Lytton Strachey. (Courtesy Frances Partridge )

**51**. Fontcreuse, home of Peter Teed and Jean Campbell. (Courtesy Sarah Bird Wright)

**52**. Peter Teed and Jean Campbell at Fontcreuse. (© Tate Archive)

**53**. La Bergère, Cassis. (Courtesy Sarah Bird Wright)

**54–5**. Cassis, photograph by Frances Partridge. (Courtesy Frances Partridge)

**56**. Duncan Grant sketching at La Bergère , 1928. (© Tate Archive)

**58**. *Window, South of France*, 1928, painting by Duncan Grant. (Bridgeman Art Library/Manchester City Art Galleries © 1978 The Estate of Duncan Grant, courtesy Henrietta Garnett)

**59**. Angelica Bell in a tree. (© Tate Archive)

**60**. Virginia Woolf, Angelica Bell, Leonard Woolf and Judith Bagenal. (© Tate Archive)

**62**. Vita Sackville-West seated in an interior. (The Harvard Theatre Collection, The Houghton Library, Harvard University, Cambridge, Massachusetts)

**63**. Vita Sackville-West seated in garden with a dog on her lap. (The Harvard Theatre Collection, The Houghton Library, Harvard University, Cambridge, Massachusetts)

**64**. Vita Sackville-West and Virginia Woolf. (The Harvard Theatre Collection, The Houghton Library, Harvard University, Cambridge, Massachusetts)

**65**. Vita in France, photographed by Virginia Woolf, or vice-versa. (From Victoria Glenddining, *Vita* (New York: Knopf, 1983))

**67** (*top*). Virginia Woolf and Vita Sackville-West seated with two dogs. (The Harvard Theatre Collection, The Houghton Library, Harvard University, Cambridge, Massachusetts)

**67** (*bottom*). Virginia Woolf and Vita Sackville-West seated with one dog. (The Harvard Theatre Collection, The Houghton Library, Harvard University, Cambridge, Massachusetts)

**68–9**. Vita Sackville-West on a mule. (The Harvard Theatre Collection, The Houghton Library, Harvard University, Cambridge, Massachusetts)

**72**. Virginia Woolf and Roger Fry in Greece, 1932. (The Harvard Theatre Collection, The Houghton Library, Harvard University, Cambridge, Massachusetts)

**74**. Roger Fry reading on a mule. (The Harvard Theatre Collection, The Houghton Library, Harvard University, Cambridge, Massachusetts)

**75**. Caricature of Roger Fry lecturing, by Walter Sickert. (Whitworth Art Gallery, University of Manchester © DACS)

**76**. Grafton Gallery exhibition poster for Manet and the Post-Impressionists.

**77**. Roger Fry with paintbox, 1910. (The Harvard Theatre Collection, The Houghton Library, Harvard University, Cambridge, Massachusetts)

**79**. Vanessa Bell and Angelica Bell Garnett. (Courtesy Angelica Bell Garnett)

**80**. Virginia Woolf, portrait by Percy Wyndham Lewis. (Bridgeman Art Library/Victoria & Albert Museum (© The Estate of Mrs G. A. Wyndham Lewis)

**82–3**. Virginia Woolf in reverie. (The Harvard Theatre Collection, The Houghton Library, Harvard University, Cambridge, Massachusetts)

**84**. Ethyl Smyth. (The Harvard Theatre Collection, The Houghton Library, Harvard University, Cambridge, Massachusetts)

**86**. (*left*) Dust jacket for *The Waves*, designed by Vanessa Bell. (The Bloomsbury Workshop © 1961 The Estate of Vanessa Bell, courtesy Henrietta Garnett)

**86**. (*right*) Dustjacket for *Three Guineas*, designed by Vanessa Bell. (The Bloomsbury Workshop © 1961 The Estate of Vanessa Bell, courtesy Henrietta Garnett)

**87**. James and Alix Strachey with Virginia Woolf (The Harvard Theatre Collection, The Houghton Library, Harvard University, Cambridge, Massachusetts)

**88**. Dorothy Strachey Bussy. (Manuscripts Department, Lilly Library, University of Indiana, Bloomington, Indiana)

**89**. Virginia Woolf with Quentin and Julian Bell. (The Harvard Theatre Collection, The Houghton Library, Harvard University, Cambridge, Massachusetts)

**92**. Example of Virginia Woolf s handwriting. (From *The Letters of Virginia Woolf*, edited by N. Nicolson and J. Trautmann, published by the Hogarth Press. Used by permission of Random House Group Ltd.)

**93**. Virginia Woolf resting her chin in cupped hand. (The Harvard Theatre Collection The Houghton Library, Harvard University, Cambridge, Massachusetts)

**95**. Virginia looking into her hat. (Manuscripts Department, Lilly Library, University of Indiana, Bloomington, Indiana)

**98**. Portrait of Lytton Strachey by Dora Carrington. (Bridgeman Art Library/Private Collection. Reproduced by courtesy of Frances Partridge)

**99**. Lytton Strachey at Ham Spray House. (Manuscripts Department, Lilly Library, University of Indiana, Bloomington, Indiana)

**100**. Dora Carrington, Ralph Partridge, Lytton and Oliver Strachey. (From C. G. Heilbrun, *Lady Ottoline's Album* (New York: Knopf, 1976), reproduced by courtesy of Carolyn Heilbrun)

**101**. Dora Carrington, photo by Lytton Strachey. (Courtesy Frances Partridge)

**103**. Portrait of J. M. Keynes by Gwen Raverat. (By courtesy of the National Portrait Gallery)

**104**. Lydia Lopokova at 46 Gordon Square. (From *The Letters of Lydia Lopokova & J. M. Keynes*, edited by P. Hill and R. Keynes (New York: Scribner's, 1989))

**105**. Charles Mauron and E. M. Forster, photo by Alice Mauron. (Modernist Library, University of Cambridge)

**106**. Charles and Marie Mauron. (© Tate Archive)

**107**. Lytton Strachey and Virginia Woolf at Garsington. (The Harvard Theatre Collection, The Houghton Library, Harvard University, Cambridge, Massachusetts)

**108**. Simon Bussy, Vanessa Bell and Duncan Grant at Garsington. (From C. G. Heilbrun, *Lady Ottoline's Album* (New York: Knopf, 1976), reproduced by courtesy of Carolyn Heilbrun)

**109**. Ottoline Morrell, portrait by Simon Bussy. (© Tate Gallery. Copyright Reserved)

**110**. A smiling Virginia Woolf at Garsington. (From C. G. Heilbrun, *Lady Ottoline's Album* (New York: Knopf, 1976), reproduced by courtesy of Carolyn Heilbrun)

**112**. Virginia Woolf with head resting on hand, photograph by Gisèle Freund. (John Hillelson/© Gisèle Freund)

**113**. Virginia Woolf smoking cigarette in holder, photograph by Gisèle Freund. (John Hillelson/© Gisèle Freund)

**114**. Virginia Woolf, photo by Man Ray. (© Man Ray Trust/ADAGP, Paris & DACS, London 2001)

**116**. Leonard Woolf with Vita Sackville-West and dogs. (The Harvard Theatre Collection, The Houghton Library, Harvard University, Cambridge, Massachusetts)

**118** (*left*). Bust of Virginia Woolf at Monk's House. (Courtesy Sarah Bird Wright)

**118** (*right*). Bust of Leonard Woolf at Monk's House. (Courtesy Sarah Bird Wright)

**121**. Virginia Woolf's writing studio. (The Harvard Theatre Collection, The Houghton Library, Harvard University, Cambridge, Massachusetts)

**122**. The elms named Leonard and Virginia at Monk's House. (The Harvard Theatre Collection, The Houghton Library, Harvard University, Cambridge, Massachusetts)

**124**. Virginia Woolf with hat on grass and statue. (The Harvard Theatre Collection, The Houghton Library, Harvard University, Cambridge, Massachusetts)

**125**. Leonard with pipe. (The Harvard Theatre Collection, The Houghton Library, Harvard University, Cambridge, Massachusetts)